THE GREAT PLAINS PHOTOGRAPHY SERIES

A HARMONY OF THE ARTS

Edited by Frederick C. Luebke

The Nebraska State Capitol

University of Nebraska Press: Lincoln & London

Copyright © 1990 by
the University of Nebraska Press
All rights reserved
Manufactured in the United States
of America

This volume in the
Great Plains Photography Series
is made possible
by a grant from the University of
Nebraska Foundation to
extend the work of the University
beyond its campuses.

The paper in this book meets the
minimum requirements
of American National Standard for
Information Sciences—
Permanence of Paper for Printed
Library Materials,
ANSI Z39.48–1984.

Library of Congress Cataloging
in Publication Data
A Harmony of the arts : the Nebra-
ska state capitol /
edited by Frederick C. Luebke.
p. cm.
Bibliography: p.   Includes index.
Contents:
The capitals and capitols of Nebra-
ska / Frederick C. Luebke –
The architectural vision of Bertram
Grosvenor Goodhue /
H. Keith Sawyers – Symbolism
and inscriptions /
David Murphy – Art, architecture,
and humanism /
Dale L. Gibbs – The decorative art of
Hildreth Meiere /
Joan Woodside and Betsy Gabb –
The capitol murals /
Norman Geske and Jon Nelson –
Landscape
architecture / Robert C. Ripley.
ISBN 0-8032-2887-2
(alk. paper). – ISBN 0-8032-7931-0
(alk. paper)
1. Nebraska State Capitol (Lincoln,
Neb.)   2. Goodhue,
Bertram Grosvenor, 1869-1924 –
Themes, motives.
3. Interior architecture – Nebraska –
Lincoln.   4. Decoration
and ornament – Nebraska – Lincoln.
5. Lincoln (Neb.) –
Buildings, structures, etc.   I. Luebke,
Frederick C., 1927-
NA4413.L56H37   1990
725'.11'09782293–dc19
89-4773   CIP

TO THE MEMORY OF **BERTRAM GROSVENOR GOODHUE** 1869–1924

Contents

Illustrations

The original idea for this book must be credited to Jon Nelson, curator of the Center for Great Plains Studies Collection of Western Art at the University of Nebraska–Lincoln. In my capacity as director of the center, I asked him to make suggestions for a public lecture series that the Center for Great Plains Studies could sponsor in the fall of 1985. His response was that Nebraskans would welcome a set of addresses on the Nebraska State Capitol, a building now a half-century old. He was right; public response matched our fondest expectations.

Nelson first got the agreement of qualified lecturers to participate in the series. Next, he put his ideas together in the form of a small-grant proposal that was submitted to the Nebraska Humanities Council. With its assistance, six weekly lectures were then presented to capacity audiences in the old Senate Chamber of the Nebraska State Capitol during September and October 1985. Nelson served as moderator for the series; the lecturers were Keith Sawyers, David Murphy, Dale Gibbs, Norman Geske, Robert Ripley, and Frederick Luebke.

The next step was to convert a series of informal, illustrated presentations into a book. Encouraged by the excellent attendance and the warm response of persons at the lectures (some of whom asked if we intended to publish them), we agreed to find the time required to complete the work.

Along the way we added another chapter. The major omission in the original lecture series was a presentation on the work of Hildreth Meiere, the artist who designed the wonderful mosaics in the capitol. It then came to our attention that Joan Woodside and Betsy Gabb, both of the University of Nebraska College of Home Economics, were working on Meiere's accomplishments. They graciously agreed to contribute a chapter on the mosaics of Hildreth Meiere.

Why a new book on the capitol? The simple fact is that nothing readily available to the public had been published in more than twenty years. Several guides of one sort or another had been produced, but decades had passed since informed, interpretive essays had appeared. Two significant articles on the capitol had been published in *Nebraska History*, but they could not meet the need for a fresh examination of this unique building fifty years after its completion.

After the lecturers had transformed their notes into chapters, it became clear to me, as editor of the volume, that one basic theme runs throughout: the contributing authors independently emphasize that the Nebraska State Capitol harmonizes a variety of artistic expressions. They describe how each of the artists— architect, symbologist, sculptor, muralist, mosaicist, landscapist—had joined to produce a unified work of art; all had been willing to serve the purposes of the building as an expression of humanistic values and aspirations. Hence I chose *A Harmony of the Arts* as the title of this book.

The idea of such an artistic collaboration was clearly in the mind of Thomas Kimball, the distinguished Nebraska architect who served as the professional adviser to the Capitol Commission appointed in 1919. But Bertram Grosvenor Goodhue, the architect chosen by the commission to design the building, became the central figure in the evolution of the concept. He selected collaborating artists with great care; he knew they shared his artistic values.

Goodhue did not know Hartley Burr Alexander before he began his Nebraska work. Alexander, a philosopher and anthropologist at the University of Nebraska, drew upon his own rich background in the humanities as he developed the symbological details of Goodhue's vision and invested the building's many inscriptions with poetic elegance. Each of the other artists—the sculptor Lee Lawrie, the mosaicist Hildreth Meiere, the landscapist Ernst Herminghaus, the several muralists plus other artists of lesser renown—brought Goodhue's grand conception to reality with their individual skills.

The Nebraska State Capitol is the product of their art. As Dale Gibbs describes it, the structure "embodies the union of art, architecture, and humanism." It is a "convincing and moving evocation of humanistic concern expressed in form, space, and detail." No ordinary building, this harmonious union of formal and symbolic expression "recognizes and celebrates the nature of man."

No attempt is made here to provide a complete inventory of the capitol sculptures, murals, and mosaics. Nor are all the artists who participated in the collaboration treated here. That is as it should be; this book is not a catalog. Instead it is a unified series of essays that aims to develop new understanding and appreciation of an important symbol in the cultural and civic lives of Nebraskans.

The publication of this book is the result of an excep-

tional measure of cooperation among several agencies of Nebraska state government. The idea originated in the Center for Great Plains Studies of the University of Nebraska–Lincoln, but it could not have come to fruition without the cooperation of the Nebraska State Department of Administrative Services and the Nebraska State Historical Society. Each of the authors is employed by one of these three agencies, but each unit has contributed also in other ways. Black and white photography has been underwritten by the Nebraska State Historical Society; most of the color illustrations have been supplied by the office of Capitol Restoration and Promotion in the Nebraska State Department of Administrative Services. Coordinating services have been provided by the Center for Great Plains Studies. It is a pleasure to acknowledge the assistance of each of these administrative units.

An art book without illustrations is an impossibility. Inevitably, the inclusion of dozens of photographic images, especially those in color, significantly increases the costs of production. Because Nebraska is a state with a low population, the likelihood of recovering such expenses from sales is slight. In order to keep the price of this book within a reasonable range, the University of Nebraska Foundation contributed substantially to its publication. Sidney Spelts, a professional photographer in Lincoln, Nebraska, gave generously of his time and energy to take most of the color photography reproduced in this book.

Editing a book of this kind is a complex task that demands a high level of cooperation from many persons. I gratefully recognize the special assistance of Robert Ripley, David Murphy, and Jon Nelson. Their generous help in editing the illustrations was essential.

FREDERICK C. LUEBKE

1

The Capitals and Capitols of Nebraska

Frederick C. Luebke

When Europeans visit the Great Plains region of the United States, they are impressed by the newness of the place. Coming from communities that often are filled with physical evidence of great age, they are reminded that here virtually none of the visible marks of Euroamerican culture are more than a mere century old. Before 1854, the year in which Nebraska was legislated into existence, permanent residence in this place was technically illegal. Except for the never-numerous Indians, a few fur trappers and traders, and some soldiers and their camp followers clustered around Fort Kearny, Nebraska had no population. It had no government, no capital city, and hence no capitol building. Yet a mere eighty years passed from that time to the dedication of Nebraska's present magnificent statehouse, the preeminent symbol of the state and the progressive spirit that in past times seemed to characterize its people.

There had been no clamor in Nebraska for the creation of a territorial government. That came instead from politicians in the national capital who wished to build a transcontinental railroad across the vast and empty spaces of the Great Plains. Recognizing the need for some sort of government in the area where the projected transportation link between East and West was to be constructed, Congress enacted the bill establishing the territories of Kansas and Nebraska in May 1854, and by the end of June treaties with Indians had opened lands along the Missouri River for private ownership. Immediately thereafter hundreds of settlers poured into the territory. Within weeks several new "towns" sprang up on the west bank of the Missouri River, including Omaha, Nebraska City, and Brownville. But only Bellevue, a few miles north of the mouth of the Platte River, bore any resemblance to a settled community before that fateful summer, when it was home to not more than fifty persons.

The Politics of Capital Location

Which settlement was to serve as the capital of the fledgling territory? No one knew for sure because the law did not specify where the seat of government was to be located. In effect, the capital would be located wherever the governor of Nebraska Territory decided to conduct the business of his office. President Franklin Pierce, in conformance with the law, appointed Francis Burt, an undistinguished politician from South Carolina, to the governorship, but Burt did not arrive until early October 1854.

In the meantime people streamed into the territory to establish more or less permanent residence. What kind of persons were they? Most were young, vigorous, aggressive; males were in the majority, though not overwhelmingly so. Few were men of means, and although most were literate, a large proportion had only the rudiments of formal education. Most were from the states directly east: Iowa, Illinois, Indiana, Ohio, and Pennsylvania. Others hailed from the South, but relatively few originated in New England or upstate New York. Immigrants from Europe, chiefly England, Ireland, and Germany, were also among the earliest Nebraskans. Most of these diverse folk came up the river from Missouri or across the river from Iowa. Often willing to take significant risks, they came to Nebraska hoping to get rich as quickly as possible and with minimal regard for the niceties of established procedures.

Nebraska's founding fathers, unlike those who gathered in Philadelphia in 1776 to declare the nation's independence, were not a distinguished group. They were ordinary people looking for ways to get ahead in a competitive world. An election was held in the autumn of 1854 to choose the first members of the territorial legislature. To no one's surprise, almost all were connected in some way with town-site specula-tion or promotion, either directly or indirectly, such as a newspaper editor of a weekly sheet created to publicize a new community and to facilitate the sale of lots. For persons of such interests, the location of the new territorial capital was a matter of supreme importance. If a person had invested much in a town—for example, Brownville—he could enhance the possibilities for success significantly by getting his town selected as the capital. In that case, his town, unlike many others founded in those hectic months, would probably survive. Growth would be virtually guaranteed; business ventures of many kinds were likely to succeed. Carpenters and masons would find much employment; storekeepers would find business brisk; printers would secure government contracts; lawyers would be attracted like bees to honey. Thus, for the first years of Nebraska's existence as a political entity, capital location was the dominant issue, just as politics was the lifeblood of territorial town-site speculators.

This was all the more so because the national political-party system was in a state of flux during the 1850s. As a matter of fact, it was the Kansas-Nebraska Act of 1854 that administered the coup de grace to the old Whig party, which then ceased to function effectively as a force in national politics. The Democratic party, though deeply split by the slavery issue, dominated national politics in the 1850s, especially in the territories, where government jobs were usually tied to loyalty to the party in power. For Nebraska in the 1850s that caused most persons interested in politics to claim membership in the Democratic party, regardless of what they might have been before they arrived in this place. More significantly, it meant that partisanship was relatively unimportant in territorial Nebraska, compared with the question of capital location.

Because the Kansas-Nebraska Act had specified

that the first territorial legislature would meet at a time and place designated by the territorial governor, the question of who this man was and what his priorities were was of crucial importance to the town-site speculators. Finally, early in October, President Pierce's appointee, Francis Burt, arrived by steamboat from St. Louis. The trip had been difficult and Burt was deathly ill. He disembarked at Bellevue, went straight to bed, and stayed there until October 16, when he roused himself sufficiently to take his oath of office. He died two days later. It was not an auspicious beginning for Nebraska.

Although Governor Burt never made his plans clear in the matter of the capital location, he almost surely intended that it was to be Bellevue. Had he lived, it is likely that Bellevue would be the capital of Nebraska today and that the city of Lincoln would not exist. But Burt died and into his office as acting governor strode the territorial secretary, a young man of twenty-five named Thomas Cuming, someone who had rather different ideas about the location of the capital.

Cuming was a journalist from Keokuk, Iowa. His appointment as territorial secretary flowed from the political influence of a group of Iowans in Washington, D.C., who were desirous for the Nebraska capital to be located immediately across the Missouri River from Council Bluffs, a town that had been in existence for several years. Several of his supporters in Washington were investors in the Council Bluffs and Nebraska Ferry Company. Obviously, if the Nebraska capital could be located in Omaha, Council Bluffs and everyone who had invested in its success would benefit significantly.

Omaha, the First Territorial Capital

So in the fall of 1854 there was much conniving, prob-ably even bribery, as Acting Governor Cuming decided that the recently elected legislators would convene, not in Bellevue, but in Omaha City, as it optimistically was called. The permanence of this new "city" was by no means guaranteed at that time; it consisted of no more than a score of buildings, including houses, saloons, stores, and so-called hotels.

Cuming's intentions are further revealed by his decisions regarding legislative districts, all of which served to strengthen Omaha at the expense of citizens living south of the Platte River. Thus, even though the population of the country south of the Platte was twice that in the area north of the river, Cuming assigned fourteen seats to Omaha and the North Platters, while the South Platters got only twelve. Similarly, Cuming's appointments to the territorial council (which functioned much like a senate) gave seven seats to the north and six to the south.

By that action, Cuming and the Iowans guaranteed that capital location would continue as a divisive issue in Nebraska politics for years to come. The next step was for the Council Bluffs and Nebraska Ferry Company to donate a hastily constructed building in Omaha to serve as the first territorial capital. Located on Ninth Street between Farnam and Douglas, the building measured seventy-five by thirty-three feet. Having two stories—the first for the use of the assembly and the second for the council—and constructed of brick, it actually was the most impressive structure in the infant city (figure 1.1).

Inevitably the first territorial legislature, stacked as it was to do the bidding of Acting Governor Cuming, followed through with the plan and named Omaha the capital. This was not done, however, without a fight, as much energy was expended to prevent it. There was an investigation of Cuming's role in the affair. Motions

1.1: Wood engraving of the first territorial capitol of Nebraska, which was erected in Omaha in 1854.

were repeatedly introduced to amend the bill that designated Omaha as the capital and to substitute the name of other cities, among them Plattsmouth, Bellevue, and Brownville. Such efforts were always defeated by one or two votes. Finally the opposition gave up and Omaha won, seven to six in the council and fourteen to eleven in the assembly.

The Second Territorial Capitol

Entirely inadequate as it was, the first capitol building was intended to serve only temporarily. In February 1855, Mark Izard, who was President Pierce's replacement for the deceased Francis Burt, assumed his duties as Nebraska's second territorial governor. It was during his administration that the second capitol was planned and constructed.

Now the founding fathers began to think in more grandiose terms as they planned a building suitable for the new and rapidly growing territory. A reasonably attractive structure done in a manner imitative of the Federal style (of which the White House in Washington and the First Bank of the United States in Philadelphia are the most celebrated examples), the second capitol was erected on a commanding site west of the business district, where it dominated the Omaha skyline (figure 1.2). Designed by a Saint Louis architect named William Rumbold, the plans called for the addition of a decorative row of classical columns. But these were never built, mostly because the building was rushed to completion in time for the 1857–58 session of the territorial legislature. Meanwhile a slight dome was added by Governor Izard, who in high frontier style claimed to have designed the entire structure.

Like so many other public buildings constructed in those frontier times, the second territorial capitol was

**1.2: The second territorial capitol
of Nebraska, erected in Omaha in
1857–58. Photograph by William
Henry Jackson, circa 1868.**

built by contractors who were either dishonest or incompetent. By 1870, after the capital had been moved to Lincoln, the hazards of occupancy were so great that the structure was condemned as unsafe, torn down, and replaced by Omaha High School.

Meanwhile the South Platte faction in the territorial legislature continued efforts to move the capital away from Omaha. At one time the legislators actually passed a bill to move the capital to a town called Douglas, which presumably was in Lancaster County. Governor Izard angrily vetoed the measure, charging that Douglas was "a floating town, not only without location but also without inhabitants." Its existence, Izard said, "seems to be confined . . . to the brain of some desperate fortune hunter, and its identity reposes in an indefinable number of certificates of stock for $500 each, neatly gotten up and handsomely executed."

In 1858 the capital fight led to a different strategy. In this instance, a majority of the legislators, mostly from south of the Platte, approved a simple motion to reconvene the next day in the village of Florence, which is now on the north side of Omaha within its city limits. But the new territorial governor, William Richardson, refused to recognize the Florentine legislature, even though it had a majority in both houses. Thus nothing came of either this removal effort or an 1859 threat by the South Platters to secede from Nebraska Territory and join Kansas. As a matter of fact, Kansas would have none of the scheme and in a constitutional convention soundly defeated a measure to annex the South Platte country.

With the advent of the Civil War in 1861, the agitation over capital location abated somewhat as the question of statehood displaced it. This prospect was raised prematurely, it seems, because federal law required a minimum population of sixty thousand. The census of 1860, however, revealed fewer than thirty thousand inhabitants in Nebraska Territory. As the Civil War ran its course, political pressure developed in Washington for the creation of new states that could be expected to support the reelection of Abraham Lincoln in 1864. Both Nevada and Nebraska territories were possibilities. In January 1864 the Nebraska territorial legislature petitioned Congress to enact a law making statehood possible; Congress responded favorably in April. Meanwhile, opposition to statehood grew, especially among Democrats, and the movement was defeated by the voters of the territory, mostly because they believed statehood would bring higher taxes.

Another major effort at statehood was mounted by Republican leaders in 1866. Employing tactics that were questionable even in that permissive era, advocates for statehood won a narrow victory in a popular election, and a proposed constitution was dispatched to Congress for approval. Congress, however, objected to a provision that limited the right to vote to whites and demanded that the restriction be removed. The legislature, technically still a territorial body but in fact elected as a branch of state government, complied by amending the document appropriately and returning it to Washington for the presidential signature. President Andrew Johnson reluctantly signed the proclamation admitting Nebraska to the Union as the thirty-seventh state on March 1, 1867.

Lincoln Becomes the State Capital

Omaha was still the capital of Nebraska as the legislature reconvened without new elections in May 1867, but not for long. Legislators from the more populous South Platte country were relentless in their determination to take the prize away from Omaha, even though on practical grounds there were no compelling reasons to do so. Even the allegedly crumbling territorial capitol, only a decade old, could have been repaired satisfactorily. Nevertheless, one of the first bills introduced in the new state legislature called for the removal of the capital from Omaha. Quickly passed by both houses and signed into law by Governor David Butler, the act specified that a commission consisting of the governor, the secretary of state, and the state auditor should select a 640-acre site on state-owned land for the new capital. Furthermore, the site was to be chosen from lands south of the Platte River, somewhere within a tract consisting of Seward County, the northern two-thirds of Lancaster County, and the southern halves of Saunders and Butler counties. Lots in the capital were to be sold to the highest bidders; the money derived from this source was to be used as a state building fund. The new law further required that the state university and agricultural college be combined as one institution located in the capital city and that the state penitentiary also be located in or near it.

An Omaha senator, believing that he might alienate Democratic votes in favor of the measure and thereby prevent the removal, successfully amended the bill to name the new capital after the recently assassinated Republican president, Abraham Lincoln. His scheme failed on June 14, 1867, as the state senate approved the capital-removal bill eight votes to five; the vote in the house of representatives was proportionately the same: twenty-five to fourteen. Omaha legislators, of course, constituted the opposition.

The capital commissioners accomplished their task with considerable speed and a certain lack of discretion. After a hasty tour of possible locations (including Ashland and Yankee Hill) that lay within the specified tract, the commissioners selected a site, not on state-owned land as the law specified, but on land donated by residents of the hamlet of Lancaster (population thirty) for the purpose. The commissioners were especially attracted by the proximity of the proposed site to well-known saline deposits that, in their mistaken opinion, offered good possibilities for commercial development, thereby affording the new capital an economic base in addition to the governmental. In fact, however, the saline basin subsequently produced more debts than profits and had the effect of forcing urban development in Lincoln south and eastward, away from lands that, until recent decades, were subject to flooding.

The sale of lots in the new capital city began a month later on September 18, 1867. The fate of Lincoln as a city, like the political prospects of its backers, was inseparably linked to the success of the auction. If sales were slow or the bids low, there would be insufficient money for the construction of the capitol. The three capital commissioners, David Butler, Thomas Kennard, and John Gillespie, were frankly worried. If Lincoln failed to come into existence as a city, the Omahans were sure to abort the removal process. The *Omaha Republican* declared that a city founded on fiat was destined to fail. "Nobody will ever go to Lincoln," it predicted, "who does not go the legislature, the lunatic asylum, the penitentiary, or some of the state institutions." Certainly it was in the interest of this newspaper to ignore the successful precedents established by the national capital in Washington and by Madison, the state capital of Wisconsin. Still, it was clear that as a city Lincoln might die at birth. As the *Republican* was pleased to point out, Lincoln lacked all the advantages offered by location on a river or a railroad.

1.3: The first state capitol of Nebraska, erected in Lincoln in 1867–68.

The results of the first sales were dreadful and produced a mere tenth of what the commissioners hoped for. Few potential buyers were willing to risk being the first to invest. Something had to be done quickly. Not above resorting to "irregularities," the commissioners secretly plotted with a group of investors from Nebraska City to force the bidding to prices higher than the appraised value of the lots. Reversing an earlier decision, they also agreed to join individually in the bidding, thereby hoping to generate new confidence in the enterprise. The logjam was thus broken and within several weeks more than fifty thousand dollars had been raised. For the moment Lincoln's future seemed assured. Thomas Kennard, for one, demonstrated his confidence in the future of Lincoln by building a lovely mansion for himself just one block east of the capitol square. Gracefully done in an Italianate Revival style, the structure stands today as a well-preserved and charming remnant of Lincoln's turbulent and uncertain beginnings.

The First State Capitol Building

Meanwhile the legislature continued to meet in Omaha as it waited for the completion of the first state capitol building on the four-block square set aside for that purpose in Lincoln. The capital commissioners advertised in several Nebraska newspapers for the submission of plans and specifications for the new structure, which was to cost forty thousand dollars. At first there was no response to their call. Finally, after the commissioners placed a notice in the *Chicago Tribune*, a submission was received from a Chicago architect named James Morris. Characterized by one historian of the time as "a fifth-rate architect," Morris proposed a structure so unattractive that, one suspects, had any other plan been submitted, his would never have been realized.

Construction of Nebraska's first state capitol began in November 1867. An ungainly building, it measured 160 by 70 feet and faced west. Its unimaginative façade was dominated by a disproportionately large tower 120 feet high (figure 1.3). Not a memorable achievement, the two-story structure was to be faced with native limestone. Since none of suitable quality could be found locally, Morris, as supervisor of construction, successfully appealed to the commissioners for permission to use stone from Gage County, some forty miles to the south. Denounced by some critics as an unwarranted extravagance, this raised the cost to more than seventy-five thousand dollars, not including an additional ten thousand dollars for furnishings. Erected in great haste by the only contractor (another Chicagoan) to submit a bid, the building was ready for occupancy in December 1868, about a month before the new legislature was to convene.

With a brand-new capitol in use, it would seem that Lincoln's inhabitants could rest assured that they had successfully weathered the storm, but the statehouse had been built so shabbily that, just like the territorial capitol in Omaha, it began to reveal its structural in-

adequacies immediately. By 1875, only seven years after its completion, it was "in danger of falling down," according to one account. To many Nebraskans this was clear evidence that Lincoln was a sink of official corruption at least as bad as Omaha. It is not surprising, therefore, that during the 1870s there were repeated efforts to remove the capital from Lincoln to a place that was presumably more centrally located in the state, such as Columbus or Kearney.

Several bills for this purpose were introduced at various times, but the Lincoln politicians always managed to play off one faction against another and kill such measures in committee. In one instance, Kearney interests were mollified with a road from their city southward to the Kansas state line; in other cases potential competitors were bought off with grants of state land for the construction of railroads.

The best way of fending off such threats was to proceed with the repair or replacement of the first capitol. In 1879, in his official message to the legislature, Governor Silas Garber reported that the north wall was in danger of collapsing, that other portions of the building were unsafe, that major repairs were necessary, and that the time had come to consider the construction of a new building large enough to house the functions of state government.

The Second State Capitol

The construction of the second state capitol was not the product of a carefully devised plan. In contrast to states, such as Illinois and Iowa, or the territory of Wyoming, all of which erected monumental structures during the 1880s that are still in use today, Nebraska built its new capitol piecemeal. It was the product of series of stopgap decisions forced upon the legislature by necessity. Like the present statehouse, it was built in stages, but under rather different circumstances. Because the old structure had a north-south orientation, east and west wings could be added to the old structure and occupied before it was razed. These two sections were separately completed by 1883 at a cost of $191,000. Construction of the central portion followed immediately. By 1889 the second state capitol was completed at an additional cost of $450,000. Altogether its total length was 320 feet. The depth of the central portion was 180 feet; that of the wings was 95.

Not an ugly building like its predecessor, this capitol was reasonably attractive, given the haphazard character of its evolution (figure 1.4). In terms of its architectural style, it may be judged at best as competent. Designed by another Chicago architect, B. H. Wilcox, it was another unimaginative manifestation of the neoclassical style patterned on the national capitol with its dominating dome. In that respect it was like virtually all the other state capitols erected in the latter part of the nineteenth century, though on a more modest scale (New York's amalgam of classical elements with the Second Empire style being a major exception). The tower, with its dome and cupola, displays the verticality or elongation typical of so much architecture of the late Victorian era. Its lower part was surrounded by a square of columns, a decorative feature that tended to distract the eye from the main part of the building. The second capitol certainly was not a distinguished structure; several of Nebraska's county courthouses of this era—the years in which the brilliant Henry Hobson Richardson dominated American architecture—are clearly superior in design.

Within two decades of its dedication this building also began to display the symptoms of the disease that afflicted most of Nebraska's public buildings in the nineteenth century: settling foundations and crumbling limestone walls. Like its predecessor, it had not been built for the ages. By the turn of the century there was general agreement in the state that it would have to be replaced soon. It was simply inadequate—too small for the many functions assigned to it.

The Third State Capitol

The movement to erect a new monumental statehouse worthy of Nebraska's aspirations received much impetus with the election of Samuel R. McKelvie as governor in November 1918 just a week before the signing of the armistice that ended World War I. A Republican, this young, aggressive, thirty-seven-year-old publisher the *Nebraska Farmer* was a classic progressive of that era. Determined to modernize everything in sight, he sought in the pages of his magazine to convert farmers from yeomanry to the latest business methods of agricultural management. Similarly, he campaigned with a promise to introduce concepts of business efficiency in state government. He was convinced that Nebraska needed a new state constitution, one that would, among other things, centralize governmental power and authority in the office of the governor. Not surprisingly, he also favored strongly the construction of a new state capitol. It was to be a memorial to the sons of Nebraska who had offered their lives in the unimaginable slaughter of the Great War.

It would be a mistake, however, to attribute the construction of Nebraska's present capitol exclusively to the leadership of this man, outstanding though he was. There was a strong consensus in its favor. Thus, when the new legislature convened in January 1919, a bill to erect a new capitol sailed through. Happily signed by Governor McKelvie, the bill became law on February 20, 1919.

In its main provisions, the act established a capitol

1.4: The second state capitol of Nebraska, erected by stages from 1880 to 1889.

commission to conduct the planning and construction of the new statehouse and levied an annual property tax of one and one-half mills per dollar of valuation to defray the cost of this grand enterprise. Appointed immediately, the commission chose the distinguished Nebraska architect Thomas R. Kimball as its professional adviser. He developed and the commission approved an elaborate procedure for a national competition that was to attract submissions from the nation's best architectural firms and, at the same time, guard carefully the anonymity of the competitors. A procedure was devised for the selection of a jury of

three distinguished American architects who were to choose the winning design.

In January 1920 the Capitol Commission issued its announcement for the final stage of competition. The commissioners were keenly sensitive to the symbolic role Nebraskans would assign to the new building. They declared that since the capitol would be "the outward sign of the character of [the state's] people," it should express "their respect for its traditions and history, their belief in its importance and worth, and their love of its fair name."

The competition stimulated a lively nationwide inter-

est and in June 1920 the jury reported its decision to the commission. The winner was "number 4," whose identity, still unknown to the jury, was Bertram Grosvenor Goodhue of New York. His design, considered to be strikingly modern by his contemporaries, represented a fascinating departure from the vocabulary architects traditionally had used for such public structures. Dispensing with columns, cornices, pediments, and all the other customary elements of neo-classical architecture, Goodhue had produced a design that, in the words of the jury, is "as free from binding traditions as it is from prejudice." Nebraskans were as pleased then as they are today.

Ground was broken on April 15, 1922, in the last year of McKelvie's two terms as governor. It was a momentous occasion. Many dignitaries, including the aging Marshal Joseph Joffre of France, who had served as commander in chief of Allied forces in World War I, were present as Governor McKelvie broke ground, not with a shovel, but with two horses drawing a plow.

A dozen years were to pass before the building was completed, but on that day in 1922 Nebraskans began what remains today a remarkable accomplishment: the construction of a capitol totally unlike its predecessors, a dignified, graceful, carefully constructed monument that expresses the values, hopes, and aspirations of its builders, as it does of the generations who have followed (figure 1.5). It is, as Nebraskans like to think, one of America's great architectural achievements of the twentieth century.

1.5: The third state capitol of Nebraska, under construction in 1928.

2

The Architectural Vision of Bertram Grosvenor Goodhue

H. Keith Sawyers

The Nebraska State Capitol is an anomaly. It is a re-markable architectural achievement that was con-ceived, designed, and constructed in an era when few outstanding buildings were erected in the United States. When viewed from a broad cultural perspec-tive, the quarter-century from 1910 to 1935 was not a period of great accomplishment in American architec-tural history. Rather, it was a time of transition accom-panied by much uncertainty, confusion, and retreat. It is not surprising therefore that the period has been neglected by architectural historians. Yet every such period has its flashes of talent, its examples of out-standing work. The Nebraska State Capitol is a no-table example.

There were few truly innovative American architects in those years. Rarely were they stimulated to rebuild America in accord with some visionary image. As a group, they generally were conservative or cautious in the practice of their profession. Architecture was usu-ally practiced by men of genteel traditions with impec-cable social credentials. Steeped in the aesthetic principles of the Ecole des Beaux-Arts in Paris, they rarely displayed the experimentalism associated with major painters of that time or the excitement that in-fused much of its great literature. This was the social context in which the Nebraska State Capitol was planned and executed.

The Nebraska Competition

As World War I ran its course it became obvious to offi-cials of the Nebraska state government that its capitol, erected in the 1880s, would have to be replaced. They decided to draw upon popular sentiment by propos-ing that a new structure be built as a memorial to young men of Nebraska who had given their lives in what they called the Great War.

Early in 1919 the state legislature approved and the

governor signed a bill that created a capitol commission, whose assigned task was "the preparation of working plans and specifications for the erection and completion, at the existing site, of a suitable building for a state capitol." The commission selected Thomas R. Kimball, a prominent Omaha architect, as its professional adviser. Subsequent events proved this a fortunate choice.

Kimball was well prepared for his task. Probably the most distinguished architect in the history of the state, Kimball was educated at the University of Nebraska. His formal training in architecture was at Massachusetts Institute of Technology, plus a stint in Paris at the Ecole des Beaux-Arts. He had designed several of Nebraska's most distinguished buildings, including St. Cecilia's Cathedral in Omaha, the Omaha Public Library, the Burlington Railroad Station in Omaha, and the Hall County Court House in Grand Island. Well known nationally, he was serving as president of the American Institute of Architects at the time of his appointment.

Since the architect of the new state capitol was to be selected by competition, Kimball's duties included the development and supervision of the selection process, as well as the preparation of the program for the building. Kimball had serious doubts about the desirability of architectural competitions. In his opinion, design programs were often excessively restrictive and therefore tended to inhibit artistic expression. For that reason, he prepared a capitol program that was remarkably free. The new structure was to be "an inspiring monument worthy of the State for which it stands; a thing of beauty, so conceived and fashioned as to properly record and exploit our civilization, aspirations, and patriotism, past, present, and future." The program did not specify that any specific style was to

be used, but it declared that the jury was to give equal weight to three "lines of judgement—the Practical, the Beautiful, and the Reasonable."

The program further required that the design should allow for the collaboration of artists: architect, sculptor, painter, and landscapist. In articulating this specification, Kimball was reflecting his commitment to the Beaux-Arts tradition, which strongly stressed the interrelationships of the various arts. Ultimately this requirement was to contribute immeasurably to the character of the final product.

At Kimball's direction, the competition was intended to select the architect rather than the scheme, so that the commission could be involved in its final development. The competition was undertaken in two phases: the first was restricted to Nebraska architects only and the second was opened to nationally prominent firms. Ten competitors were finally selected. The Nebraska entrants were Ellery Davis of Lincoln, John Latenser of Omaha, and John and Alan McDonald of Omaha. The national entrants were H. Van Buren Magonigle, Bertram Goodhue, John Russell Pope, Tracy and Swartwout, and McKim, Mead, and White, all of New York City; Bliss and Faville of San Francisco; and Paul Cret of Philadelphia.

The jury consisted of three leading architects. The law specified that the commission was to select one, the competitors would collectively choose a second, and the third would be picked "by the two thus chosen." The commissioners chose Waddy B. Wood of Washington, D.C., who was well known for his Beaux-Arts designs for banks, embassies, and commercial buildings. The competitors selected James Gamble Rogers of New York, a highly successful architect trained at Yale and in Paris. Wood and Rogers in turn designated as the third juror Willis Polk of San Fran-

2.1: Nebraska State Capitol competition, front elevation, design submitted by H. Van Buren Magonigle of New York.

cisco, another influential architect of the Beaux-Arts school. As a condition of the competition, Kimball indicated that the identities of the jurors would not be revealed until after their decision had been announced, in order to prevent the competitors from appealing to known design prejudices.

Still, all of the persons involved in selecting the winner shared a common training and tradition; the career of each reveals commitment to Beaux-Arts design principles, including the belief that classical forms— columns, domes, pediments, porticoes, pilasters, and monumental staircases—were particularly appropriate, if not virtually required, in the designs for government buildings. Equally significant was the fact that the powerful symbol of the United States Capitol continued to dominate the thinking of both professional architects and the general public in 1920. The culture

seemed to dictate that governmental functions were to be housed in classical buildings.

It is no surprise therefore that most of the competitors submitted designs that were unswervingly loyal to the classical tradition as espoused by the Ecole des Beaux-Arts. This is particularly evident in the solution submitted by Van Buren Magonigle (figure 2.1). Having studied for two years in Rome, he proposed to reproduce its architecture here. His design was an ordered complex on a vast scale in which everything is symmetrical. The central building with its large halls was to contain the legislative chambers; the semi-detached northeast and northwest blocks were to house the judicial and executive branches, respectively. It was a grand plan and although it adhered closely to classical formulas, it was not without imaginative elements.

A PROPOSED CAPITOL FOR THE STATE OF NEBRASKA IN THE CITY OF LINCOLN

The scheme proposed by John Russell Pope was highly favored by the jury and was a strong competitor until the final selection was made (figure 2.2). Clearly modeled on the national capitol in Washington, Pope's design is compact compared to Magonigle's. Perfect symmetry and good proportions are retained in this proposal, which adheres rigidly to all the classical formulas.

Much the same must be said for the solution proposed by John Latenser. Latenser, who was born in Liechtenstein and educated in Germany, is well known in Nebraska as the architect of the Douglas County Court House and Omaha Central High School. His classical design closely adhered to the commonly accepted pattern in American capitol design, as did the scheme submitted by the McDonalds of Omaha. Their adherence to Beaux-Arts traditions is evident in a large, formal site plan that included a two-block-long esplanade extending northward from the main structure and terminating in a garden bounded by a matched pair of office buildings.

The firm of Bliss and Faville presented a plan for a compact structure with a somewhat austere exterior. Although it fails to incorporate a pediment, it remains well within the Beaux-Arts tradition. The building appears to be rather small and lacking in sophistication compared to the other proposals.

The personal histories of the principal partners in the Tracy and Swartwout firm are reflected in the design they submitted for the Nebraska capitol. Both Evarts Tracy and Egerton Swartwout were educated at Yale and both had worked for McKim, Mead, and White, then the most famous architectural firm in the United States. Their solution bears a resemblance to the Missouri State Capitol, which they had designed just a few years earlier (figure 2.3). Striving for architectural grandeur, they proposed a dome rather too large for the rest of the building. Much formal landscaping was also part of this ambitious scheme, which included a grandiose exterior courtyard. True to Beaux-Arts principles, rigorous symmetry pervades both the proposed building and its landscape setting.

2.2: Nebraska State Capitol competition, front elevation, design submitted by John Russell Pope of New York.

2.3: Nebraska State Capitol competition, front elevation, design submitted by the architectural firm of Tracy and Swartwout of New York.

2.4: Nebraska State Capitol competition, front elevation, design submitted by Ellery Davis of Lincoln, Nebraska.

2.5: Nebraska State Capitol competition, front elevation, design submitted by the architectural firm of McKim, Mead, and White of New York.

2.6: Nebraska State Capitol Competition, front elevation, design submitted by Paul Cret of Philadelphia.

Like all the others, the design submitted by Ellery Davis of Lincoln also reveals a commitment to classicism (figure 2.4). Davis, who was educated at Nebraska and Columbia, proposed an austere elevation with all the typical classical elements. His design is conventional in every respect, save for the radical gesture of a huge tower. The idea was innovative but its execution, when compared with the winning design, was less graceful.

The New York firm of McKim, Mead, and White was the most distinguished promoter of Beaux-Arts classicism in the United States at the time. By 1919, however, each of the principal partners had either died or retired, yet the firm's commitment to the classical tradition for important public buildings persisted. Horizontality is a distinctive feature of this vast scheme, which employs a low dome of rather awkward proportions (figure 2.5). Another distinctive element is an obelisk intended as a memorial to the slain soldiers of the re-

cent world war. The scale of the plan was gigantic and would have required the use of at least six additional city blocks for the main complex, plus four more for an esplanade stretching northward and lined with office buildings. This entry was eventually granted third place by the jurors.

The proposal submitted by Paul Cret is similar to the winning design in that it tends to deemphasize classical details more than most other entries (figure 2.6). Horizontality is again dominant, as in the McKim, Mead, and White scheme, and the dome remains only in an abstracted form. A large memorial obelisk with the graceful proportions of the Washington Monument dominates a formal garden enclosed on three sides by the structure. Refreshing though the Cret design is, it fell short of the bold originality, the harmonious proportions, and the striking monumentality of the plan offered by Bertram Goodhue.

The Winning Architect: Bertram Goodhue

The architect who submitted the winning design for the capitol was Bertram Grosvenor Goodhue. Born in Connecticut in 1869 into a family of modest means, Goodhue was unlike many of the better-known architects of his day. Unable to attend Yale University, as had some of his more prosperous ancestors, he never had formal training in architecture—at Yale, in Paris, or anywhere else. Instead, he followed a practical course as a draftsman that led him, at the young age of twenty-two, into partnership with the firm of Cram and Wentworth in Boston. A few years later, upon the death of Charles Wentworth, the company was reorganized as Cram, Goodhue, and Ferguson, a fruitful association that lasted fifteen years.

Despite this success, Goodhue suffered the torments of one who felt excluded from the fraternity of his peers. He was obviously capable, independent, and self-reliant, yet his lack of formal training made him defensive among his colleagues. He yearned for the distinction of an academic credential and was deeply gratified when, in 1911, Trinity College of Hartford, Connecticut, granted him an honorary doctor of science degree (figure 2.7).

A complex man, Goodhue was torn between opposing tendencies in his personality. He seemed devoted to architectural principles, yet was skeptical of binding stylistic rules. He was an idealist whose designs were modified significantly by the practical problems that all architects encounter. His upbringing had liberated his fertile mind, enabling him to range widely and to draw on the humanities freely, but it also hobbled him with doubts about his talent and with fears of financial insecurity. He was both pragmatic and romantic, cautious one moment and reckless another.

Goodhue was influenced deeply by his more famous partner, Ralph Adams Cram. Six years older than Goodhue, Cram was known as the most aggressive advocate of Gothic Revival architecture in the United States. This trend was part of the Oxford Movement, which originated in England in the nineteenth century. Espousing the return to High Church theology and Catholic traditions among Anglicans in England and Episcopalians in the United States, its consequences for architecture were to stimulate a widespread return to church styles of earlier times, especially the Gothic.

Much of the partnership's success, indeed its reputation, was built upon a series of commissions executed in the Gothic manner. Of course, Goodhue shared his senior partner's biases in this regard. The professional relationship between them is clear. Cram was the theoretician who wrote and lectured extensively; he articulated the philosophical foundations of their work and pursued its cultural implications. It was Goodhue's special task to translate the firm's ideas and intentions into evocative drawings and later into built form.

A study of Goodhue's early designs reveal three basic principles. First, like his contemporary, Frank Lloyd Wright, Goodhue believed that architecture must be organically united with its landscape or setting. Second, he relied on unpretentious vernacular forms, often geometrically simple, for the primary inspiration for his designs. Third, like many of his Victorian predecessors, he incorporated towers into his compositions. A potent architectural device, the tower has served for centuries as a dramatic marker to enhance the structure that lies at its base.

These principles may be observed in a representative example of Goodhue's skill. Executed in 1910–14,

2.7: Bertram Grosvenor Goodhue in 1911, when he received an honorary doctorate from Trinity College, Hartford, Connecticut.

the Chapel of the Intercession in New York City's Trinity Cemetery provided an ideal setting for the romantic Goodhue. Mature trees, old gravestones, and an abiding sense of melancholy enhance this picturesque assemblage of timbered halls, quiet cloisters, and, inevitably, a tower.

Although much of the firm's work early in the twentieth century drew on English precedents, there were exceptions. One of the most notable was the commission to design the Panama-California Exposition in San Diego in 1911. Here Goodhue drew upon Spanish antecedents as he skillfully integrated landscape and architecture. Goodhue's independence of mind is revealed by his readiness to abandon Beaux-Arts formalism (which had been the organizing principle of virtually all preceding fairs of this kind) for a scheme

2.8: The Rockefeller Chapel, University of Chicago, Chicago, Illinois. Designed by Bertram Goodhue shortly before the Nebraska State Capitol, this structure was erected from 1918 to 1928.

2.9: Front elevation of Bertram Goodhue's design for the National Academy of Sciences building, Washington, D.C., constructed 1919–24.

based on a more variegated and natural order. His design was so successful that it launched a revival of Spanish Colonial style that spread throughout California and eventually eastward to many other parts of the United States.

Goodhue increasingly displayed a tendency toward innovation in his designs that ultimately contributed to the dissolution in 1914 of his partnership with the more conservative Cram and Ferguson. During the war years that followed, Goodhue searched for a new, more personal expression. His church designs, most notably the Rockefeller Chapel at the University of Chicago (1918–28), reveal his ongoing effort to integrate purposeful ornamentation with traditional styles (figure 2.8). But it is his public buildings that show him grappling with profound challenges to his customary work.

Goodhue's scheme for the National Academy of Sciences in Washington (1919–24) was an especially significant prelude to his design for the Nebraska State Capitol (figure 2.9). The Washington project, however, proved to be particularly frustrating for Goodhue as he confronted the unfamiliar challenge of designing a monumental structure in a monumental setting. Moreover, his relationship with the building commission was stormy. The commissioners wanted an academically correct design; Goodhue wanted a more romantic expression. The result was a compromise that is bland and lacking in conviction, but the experience convinced Goodhue that monumental architecture did not have to be dry and sterile and that it could be interpreted in personal and innovative ways. The stage was thus set for Goodhue's greatest achievement: the design for the Nebraska State Capitol.

2.10: Front elevation of the design for the Nebraska State Capitol submitted by Bertram Goodhue of New York.

2.11: Preliminary study of the Nebraska State Capitol, north side, by James Perry Wilson, an associate of Bertram Goodhue. In this drawing Goodhue's original design for the main entrance has been modified to appear much like what was actually built.

Goodhue's Winning Design

Perhaps the most striking aspect of Goodhue's plan for the capitol is the conspicuous absence of the traditional elements of classical design (figure 2.10). It offers none of the usual pediments, columns, pilasters, cornices, and porticoes that pervade the architecture of public buildings of that time. This is not to say that Goodhue also cast all Beaux-Arts principles aside. The balance and symmetry one expects of such designs remains; his use of traditional Beaux-Arts axes is simple and direct, though he did not adhere slavishly to them. He even included a few columns with non-traditional capitals in his designs for some interior halls. What the jurors recognized in Goodhue's scheme was an individuality or independence of mind that was missing in most of the other entries.

Although no records of the jury's deliberations remain, it is known that the final choice was between

John Russell Pope's proposal for a classical domed structure and Goodhue's tower-dominated entry. The jurors thus narrowed their choice in a way that reflected the basic question then confronted by American architects: Should the architecture of public buildings be founded on tradition or innovation? Goodhue's answer offered both.

The choice of Goodhue as the architect was daring and dramatic. It was due partly to that fact that both Goodhue and the jurors were influenced strongly by the criteria outlined by Thomas Kimball. Because Kimball had prescribed no specifics in style, Goodhue was free to approach the problem from his own evolving point of view, which, unlike those of his competitors, was no longer dominated by Beaux-Arts principles. Instead of contemplating the seven hills of ancient Rome, Goodhue studied the plains of Nebraska and the character of its people. Tired of imitation, he was ready for creation.

The central and most dramatic element of Goodhue's scheme is the tower (figure 2.11). More than any other part of his design, it invests the capitol with power and dignity. Although Goodhue had included towers in many of his earlier works, his use of the concept for a monumental government building was a radical innovation at that time. From a distance, one views it as a bold visual element that rises from the monotonous prairie. Towers have fascinated builders for thousands of years, imbued as they are with historical meanings. But it was only toward the end of the nineteenth century that advances in steel skeleton-frame technology had made an awesomely tall building, the skyscraper, possible. Goodhue had hoped to erect his tower in the traditional manner without steel framing, but his engineers quickly convinced him that that would be impossible.

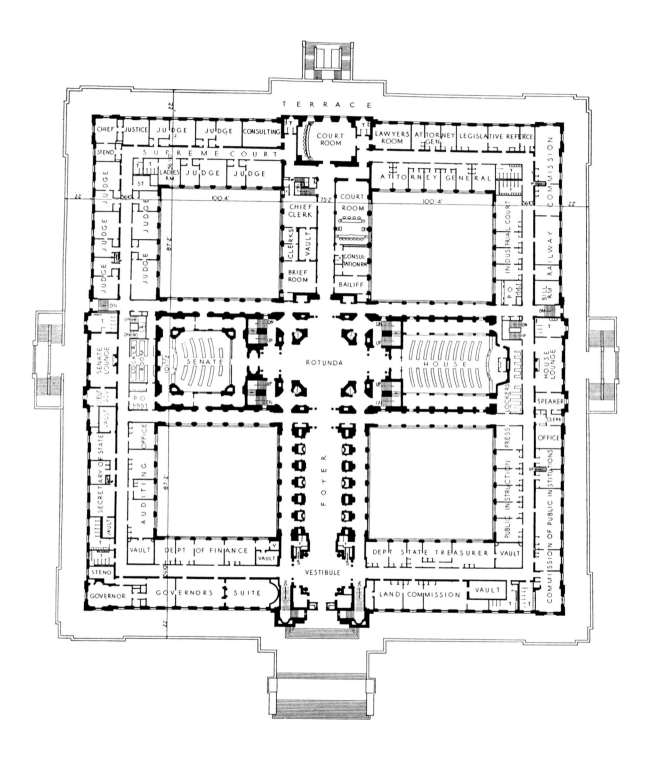

2.12: The plan of the second (main) floor of the Nebraska State Capitol reveals its cruciform configuration and the relationship of the nave-like foyer to the vestibule and the rotunda.

2.13: Drawing of the foyer looking south toward the rotunda, by Austin Whittlesey, a Goodhue associate, suggests the cathedral-like character of this space.

Symbols of economic power and success, towers used for commercial purposes at the turn of the century were universally recognized as visible expressions of ascendancy and strength. Goodhue could not have chosen a form that was at once both more traditional and modern. It was in perfect harmony with American culture in the early twentieth century.

At the same time, the tower was in harmony with requirements of economy and practicality. Unlike the designs that incorporated great domes enclosing vast interior spaces, Goodhue's tower created space that could be used. At first he thought it could be used for library stacks, but later he converted it to governmental offices.

Even though the tower dominates the design, the dome remains an integral part of Goodhue's plan. In Western culture, domes long have been associated with royal tombs and commemorative monuments, with death and immortality. Furthermore, in the United States people have tended to associate domes with capitols and government buildings. These two traditional perceptions of the dome were appropriate here because the new capitol was to function both as a memorial honoring Nebraska's dead soldiers and as the seat of government.

But it remained for Goodhue to propose a solution that was again both traditional and innovative. He capped his modern skeleton-frame tower with a small dome of conventional proportions that one reads as a symbol of both the capitol and the mausoleum. Under the dome, at the top of the tower, Goodhue placed a memorial hall. It encloses a tasteful octagonal space that is appropriate for meditation, not for pompous or overblown speeches to be delivered in some huge chamber that might have been made part of the plan at ground level.

Goodhue's scheme for the interior was less innovative than that for the exterior (figure 2.12). In this case the central design element is closely related to the cruciform configurations characteristic of his earlier church plans. The space created by the main entrance, which is on the north side of the building, functions like a vestibule; it leads directly to the Great Hall, or foyer, which has the appearance of a nave (figure 2.13, compare figure 3.11). Directly beyond it is the central crossing of the cruciform, with its high domed interior (the rotunda). The legislative chambers, the House to the right and the Senate to the left, form the transepts of this secular cathedral. Beyond the crossing is the chancel, which leads to the Supreme Court chambers in what might be thought of as the apse. The passageways that bridge the interior space at the central crossing serve as rood screens, as found in many English cathedrals. Thus, all the major elements of a church plan in Western culture are present, save the altar.

The integration of architecture with its site was another of Goodhue's design purposes. Most of the other plans submitted for the new capitol were developed along axes of unequal importance; they offered elevations that were clearly fronts or rears or sides. But Goodhue's scheme is square; it respects the inherent biaxial character of the gridiron plan. Although the four sides of his building are by no means identical, they are all similar. Moreover, Goodhue's grid plan was comfortably consonant with the surrounding city blocks, which were so typical of prairie towns such as Lincoln. Instead of contrasting rudely with its surroundings, Goodhue's capitol blends with the neighborhood, despite its monumentality, as it casually acknowledges all four points of the compass.

Goodhue's design was also entirely consonant with Kimball's prescription for the integration of the arts. Although the details remained to be worked out, Goodhue was eager to collaborate with other artists to unify sculptures, mosaics, and landscaping, as well as inspirational quotations, into a grand harmony. Another attractive feature of Goodhue's plan was the incorporation of four internal courtyards, all open to the sky and all functioning as integral parts of the large design. They made possible natural lighting for all offices in the main part of the building.

Finally, the jurors probably were attracted by the practicality of Goodhue's plan. More pragmatic in temperament and training than his peers, Goodhue revealed a sensitivity to concerns for utility and economy. The jurors, who believed Pope's plan would be the most expensive to build, thought Goodhue's was comparatively modest in scale. "He has been able to produce a building," they noted, "that is less than seventy-five percent of the size of the average building in this competition." Furthermore, Goodhue was the sole entrant who took into consideration the cost of housing state employees while construction was to be under way. By creating a design that could be built around the existing state capitol, he made it possible for the government to save several hundred thousand dollars (a huge sum in the 1920s) in rent for temporary quarters.

Goodhue's solution was to phase construction so that the north and south sections were constructed first. The next step was to vacate the old capitol and move into the new quarters, making it possible to raze the old building and to proceed with the construction of the east and central sections, followed by the tower. The final phase was to complete the west section, which presently houses the state's unicameral legislature.

After the jury decision in June selecting Goodhue's design as the winner, the Capitol Commission signed a contract in November 1920. Minor alterations were subsequently made in the plan, the most notable being a modification of the north façade and the main entrance. In this case a huge lintel supported by two huge columnlike elements was replaced with a large rounded arch that repeats at entry level the contours of the dome that towers four hundred feet above (compare figures 2.10 and 2.11). It encases a rectangular door surmounted by a sculptured frieze and a semicircular window (figure 3.9). Meanwhile, appropriate steps were taken to secure the services of the best possible collaborating artists.

Ground was broken in April 1922. Before the end of the year, contracts were let and construction began. Tragically, Bertram Goodhue died two years later at the age of fifty-five, long before the building was completed.

In December 1924 the old state capitol was vacated as government offices were moved into the first sections of the new building. Construction of the tower began in 1928. Two years later the final section was under way. Finally, in 1932, the structure was completed, furniture and furnishings were installed, and the landscaping of the grounds was begun.

It had taken Nebraska a decade to finish its magnificent new capitol, but the task had been accomplished without incurring a debt. Erected on a pay-as-you-go plan based on annual property levies, it imposed no crushing tax burden. The project was intended to cost $5,000,000, but the final bill totaled $9,770,000, not including the cost of murals, tower illumination, courtyard fountains, and a variety of other minor expenses. Because the building was occupied gradually over a period of years, Nebraskans were not conscious of a completion date. Curiously, therefore, no formal dedication ceremonies were scheduled in 1932. Not until a half-century later was this oversight remedied.

Goodhue's greatest work was conceived and constructed in a turbulent period of transition in architectural history. More than most of his contemporaries, Goodhue understood that architecture was moving into a new era that would have no tolerance for historical classicism, romanticism, and sentimentality; he knew that Beaux-Arts traditionalism was in its death throes. By 1920 several of the early examples of modernism had already been built. Goodhue sought to develop a new architecture that might occupy ground between the dead historicism of the past and the unforgiving dominance of modernism. Within five years of Goodhue's death, the world witnessed the creation of Walter Gropius's Bauhaus (1925), Ludwig Mies van der Rohe's Barcelona Pavilion (1929), and Le Corbusier's Villa Savoy (1929), which collectively defined the architecture of the next several decades.

The Nebraska State Capitol was caught in that transition. Although Nebraskans have never wavered in their appreciation for Goodhue's accomplishment, architectural historians have tended to be more restrained, describing it with respect and even admiration, but rarely with enthusiasm. Goodhue's way seemed to lead down a dead-end street; it was an anomaly. In more recent years, however, the architectural climate has changed again. We have moved into a postmodern era that often disdains modernism as harsh, sterile, monotonous, and unimaginatively geometric—afflicted by an orthodoxy as limiting as any style that preceded it. Our times offer new opportunities to learn from Goodhue's legacy. The seeds of his message may finally germinate on fertile ground.

HE WHO WOULD DULY ENQUIRE ABOUT THE BEST FORM OF THE STATE OUGHT FIRST TO DETERMINE WHICH IS THE MOST ELIGIBLE LIFE / MEN SHOULD NOT THINK IT SLAVERY TO LIVE ACCORDING TO THE RULE OF THE CONSTITUTION FOR IT IS THEIR SALVATION / LAWS AND CONSTITUTIONS SPRING FROM THE MORAL DISPOSITIONS OF THE MEMBERS OF THE STATE / LAW AND ORDER DELIVER THE SOUL / A COMMUNITY LIKE AN INDIVIDUAL HAS A WORK TO DO

No state capitol in America incorporates history and identity of place in a more comprehensive and integrated fashion than Nebraska's statehouse. This is due first to the vision of Thomas Kimball, the professional adviser to the Capitol Commission, who specified in his program for the architectural competition that a harmony of the arts was to infuse the design of the new building. Second, it is attributable to Bertram Grosvenor Goodhue, who as the winning architect was eager to achieve such unity. But the person who developed the ideas and carried them out in the symbolism and inscriptions of the capitol was Hartley Burr Alexander, who, like Kimball, was a Nebraskan.

Alexander was a latecomer to the project. He was not enlisted as a collaborator until 1921, when Goodhue, working with Lee Lawrie, the sculptor, experienced difficulties in developing inscriptions for the main entrance, located on the north side. Because it was his responsibility to guide the work of the collaborating sculptors, painters, and landscapists, Goodhue wrote to Kimball and the Capitol Commission, asking for help. Intending to integrate major attributes of governmental law into his design for the portal, Goodhue had identified three—"Knowledge, Mercy, and Force"—and needed a fourth. Shortly thereafter he wrote the commission again, indicating that there were to be many inscriptions and that, although it was possible for them to be prepared by either Goodhue or the commissioners, it would be preferable that the selection of historical quotations or the expression of exalted sentiments in dignified language be assigned to a person trained in the literary arts.

At first the commission requested that Goodhue be the one to prepare the inscriptions, but the architect, untrained in this field, continued to experience difficulties. The commission thereupon decided to appoint as a collaborator Professor Hartley Burr Alexander,

During the next ten days, Alexander concentrated on all the other inscriptions that had been prescribed for various places on the building and submitted them to Goodhue, who was much impressed. Some time later, the commission asked Goodhue to consider including several additional inscriptions. He agreed to include them, provided they met Alexander's standards of quality.

The collaboration between Goodhue and Alexander reached a new level of development in November 1922. While reviewing the sculptural model for the bison panels that flank the main entrance, Alexander criticized the design developed by Goodhue and Lawrie. Their plan called for a winged buffalo in bas-relief. Alexander objected to the idea because there was no such animal in Plains Indian mythology. Goodhue was initially disheartened and tried to defend its use on aesthetic grounds. But after Alexander responded with a detailed explanation of his criticism, Goodhue conceded and asked Alexander to supply him with additional information. As a result, Lawrie redesigned the animal as it appears today (figure 3.2). This exchange led to other consultations about the sculptural program and by September 1923, Alexander was a full partner in the development of the entire symbological program, having won the respect of both the architect and the commission.

who was chairman of the Department of Philosophy at the University of Nebraska in Lincoln. Alexander enthusiastically accepted the appointment. He quickly transformed Goodhue's clumsy "Knowledge, Mercy, and Force" into the more elegant and poetic "Wisdom, Justice, Power, and Mercy." These words, together with Lee Lawrie's symbolic sculptures, grace the majestic north entrance today (figure 3.1).

Hartley Burr Alexander

Who was this philosopher who made such an important contribution to the symbolism of the capitol? Alexander was born in Lincoln in 1873, just a few years after the city was founded. However, he grew up in Syracuse, which is about thirty-five miles east of Lincoln. His father was a self-educated Methodist minister from New England, his stepmother an artist of local

3.1: The north entrance, showing the inscription on the face of the east balustrade and the engaged sculptures on the pylon.

3.2: One of the four bison panels flanking the staircase at the north entrance.

BORN OF THE EARTH
AND TOUCHED BY THE DEEP BLUE SKY
OUT OF THE DISTANT PAST I CAME UNTO YOU
YOUR MOTHER CORN

3.3: Hartley Burr Alexander as a young man.

3.4: The Nebraska State Capitol as observed from a distance of several blocks.

distinction. Together they provided their son with a rich cultural environment. After graduating from the University of Nebraska in 1897 and teaching for a year, he attended the University of Pennsylvania and then Columbia University, which granted him a doctorate in philosophy in 1901. He worked as an editor of scholarly materials until 1908, when he eagerly accepted an appointment to a professorship in philosophy at the University of Nebraska. His involvement in the capitol project led to his appointment in 1928 to the faculty of Scripps College in Claremont, California, where he remained until his death in 1939 (figure 3.3).

A prolific writer and lecturer, Alexander understood mankind holistically. His interests ranged widely; he worked not only in philosophy but also in anthropology, poetry, and symbology. He was particularly attracted by North American Indian art, lore, and mythology and published extensively in these fields. Poetry was one of his greatest loves, and some of his poems were published in leading magazines of the time. Thus Alexander was uniquely talented to contribute in a remarkable way to the harmony of the arts embodied in the Nebraska State Capitol.

Alexander's Symbolic Scheme for the Capitol

Having been made one of the collaborating artists, Alexander developed two themes around which he organized the symbolism to be made part of the capitol's architecture. The first, which is found on the exterior of the building, recapitulates the history of law from the earliest times to modern democracy as experienced in Nebraska and the world. It also includes sculptures of major figures in that history and symbolizes their contributions to it. The second theme, which is developed mostly in the interior of the building, is more abstract. It celebrates human habitation on the plains of Ne-

braska and the relationship of civilization to the natural environment.

Alexander's conceptual scheme is related to the external environment as the context for the capitol and its formal composition. The horizontal part of the building, two stories high, forms the base for the tower and its powerful vertical sweep. As Goodhue intended, the plan of the capitol (and the four city blocks on which it is situated) is in harmony with the larger geometric grid of the city and the rectangular survey system that is imposed on the land by federal legislation. The long, low base of the capitol thus emulates the broad horizontality of Nebraska's vast, flat landscape. The tower, which contrasts so strongly with the base, was designed as a landmark that can, in fact, be observed from miles around (figure 3.4).

Alexander understood the significance of the composition completely; it was his point of departure for his entire symbolic scheme. He described it this way:

The exterior of the capitol falls into two major units, the peripheral Square and the central Tower. Their architectural forms naturally suggest their related significance in a monumental sense. The circuit of the Square is emblematic of the quarters of the Earth and the historic course of human experience. The Tower, in its upward sweep, serves as a gnomon of the Heavens and symbol of the more abstract conceptions of life derived from historical experience. Unitedly they express that combination of action and thought which is the essence of all human life, social as well as individual.

Alexander thus interpreted the formal relationship of base to tower as an expressive progression from the earthly to the heavenly, from the historical to the symbolic, and from the concrete to the abstract. It was to serve as the foundation for his entire symbolic program. He followed this splendid conception throughout.

The Exterior: A History of Law

To follow the hierarchy of meaning that undergirds Alexander's conception, we must begin a tour at the massive north portal, remembering that the horizontal base derives its meaning from historical experience and that the tower symbolizes the ascent to higher levels of the spirit.

As we approach the portal on the monumental staircase, we first confront two huge pylons that flank the entrance arch. Above the arch we read Alexander's powerful inscription (figure 3.1):

WISDOM JUSTICE POWER MERCY
CONSTANT GUARDIANS OF THE LAW

The inscription and the four figures that symbolize these attributes of law introduce the theme of the exterior tour: "The History of Law." The sequence begins at the north entrance and moves horizontally from left to right around the entire building. The subject matter progresses from ancient to modern times.

The lowest design element reminds us of the most concrete aspect of state government, the counties, which represent the democratic foundations of state law at the local level. The names of all ninety-three counties in Nebraska occupy a frieze immediately below the cornices on the four walls of the capitol.

As we move upward, we come to the next design element. Above the cornice and set on slightly projecting planes are a series of eighteen bas-relief panels that collectively represent the history of law, with each sculpture depicting a key event in the legal tradition of Western civilization (figure 3.5). The sequence is divided into two halves, with nine panels on the west side of the capitol treating ancient history and a sec-

3.5: An example of an inscribed county name showing its relationship to one of the panels on the history of law. The panel, depicting "Deborah Judging Israel," is on the west side at the northwest corner.

3.6: The pavilion on the south side of the Nebraska State Capitol, showing the staircases, the balustrade with bas-relief panels, and engaged sculptures on the pylon.

ond set of nine on the east treating modern history. The ancient series begins at the northwest corner of the capitol on the north side, continues across the west side, and ends at the southwest corner on the south side. This sequence depicts Hebrew, Greek, and Roman contributions to the law. It includes panels that represent the Old Testament conceptions of theocratic, inspired, and royal law; the founding of democracy and republicanism in Athens and Rome; and the interpretation of law through philosophy.

The modern sequence of panels commences at the southeast corner of the capitol on the south wall, continues along the eastern side of the building, and ends on the north side of the northeast corner. The panels of this series treat the founding of English law: the defense of liberty by John Milton and Edmund Burke; the acquisition of rights for the white, red, and black races in North America; and events that impinge on the legal history of Nebraska, including the Louisiana Purchase, the Kansas-Nebraska Act, and Nebraska statehood.

The large pavilion on the south side separates the ancient and modern sequences and provides an interlude in the progression of legal history (figure 3.6). Behind the pavilion are the Supreme Court chambers and the Law Library. For that reason, Alexander chose to celebrate the great historical documents on which

The figures in this interlude represent the great legislators of the ancient Western world, each embracing symbols indicative of their contributions. The arrangement is temporal, beginning with Hammurabi and continuing with Moses, Akhnaton, Solon, Solomon, Julius Caesar, Justinian, and Charlemagne. Two more figures face the interior courts. They are Napoleon, whom Alexander described as the modernizer of European law, and Minos, the legendary king of Crete and mythical judge of the dead.

Our tour next takes us to the tower, where the emphasis now shifts from historical figures and events to idealism. We begin at the base of the tower. Here eight figures, two on each side, support the tower to symbolize the fact that present-day ideals are rooted in a living past. Again the figures are in historical sequence, beginning at the west side of the north face and moving counterclockwise around the tower to the east side. Representing the genius of human civilization as embodied in the heroes of great epochs, the figures recapitulate spiritual aspects of human history, beginning with "The Dawn of History," characterized by the Egyptian scribe Pentaour, and ending with "The Liberation of Peoples," symbolized by Abraham Lincoln, the Great Emancipator (figure 3.7).

The symbolism of the base having been established in this way, the tower then rises unobstructed to great heights of abstraction and spirituality. At the octagonal drum of the dome Alexander decided to incorporate a simple but highly abstract symbol: the thunderbird (figure 3.8). This Indian symbol of the heavens and the life that the heavens bring to the earth decorates the eight panels of the base in a repetitive colored mosaic pattern. Above them the golden dome separates the structure from the blue sky. The climax of the design comes with the huge, allegorical figure of

3.7: Engaged sculptures on the north side of the tower. The series of eight figures begins on the right with Pentaour, an Egyptian scribe who represents "The Dawn of History," and ends on the left with Abraham Lincoln as a symbol for "The Liberation of Peoples."

3.8: The dome of the Nebraska State Capitol with the thunderbird designs at its base.

American political liberty rests. A triptych depicting the Declaration of Independence, the Magna Carta, and the United States Constitution is carved into the balustrade outside the Law Library (compare figure 4.2). It is set off from the historical sequence by its vertical location on the wall and in its type of sculpture. Above the balustrade in an elevated position at the top of the pavilion are eight engaged figures flanking an inscription:

POLITICAL SOCIETY EXISTS

FOR THE SAKE OF NOBLE LIVING

monumental spaces within. Like the first tour, this one follows a similar sequential pattern of rising from concrete experience to abstract principles. The faces of the two entrance balustrades bear two brief poetic statements composed by Alexander. On the left we read: HONOUR TO / PIONEERS / WHO BROKE / THE SODS / THAT MEN / TO COME / MIGHT LIVE (figure 3.1). And on the right: HONOUR TO / CITIZENS / WHO BUILD / AN HOUSE / OF STATE / WHERE MEN / LIVE WELL.

In this way Alexander established an introductory hierarchy, honoring the past on the left and the present on the right. On the sides of the balustrades are sculptural and inscriptive panels to commemorate the people who occupied the land before us. Powerful bas-relief bison celebrate Indian life (see figure 3.2). Each panel bears an inscription penned by Alexander but derived from Pawnee, Sioux, or Navaho ritual and lore. The names of Nebraska tribes are also inscribed within the panels.

Next, Alexander confronts us with a bold inscription above the main entrance, just below a panel that depicts pioneers with oxen drawing a covered wagon. Not a quotation, the statement was composed by Alexander: THE SALVATION / OF THE STATE IS / WATCHFULNESS / IN THE CITIZEN (figure 3.9). The panel and the inscription work together in repeating the honors extended to pioneers and citizens on the balustrades below.

As we pass through the doors into the vestibule, we come to a different world: an interior, a totally embracing, artificial world (figure 3.10). Three interior spaces—vestibule, foyer, and rotunda—are here treated in a unified way. We naturally anticipate other patterns of sequential and hierarchical thought, but here Alexander's program becomes doubly complex.

the Sower, mounted atop the dome, casting abroad the seeds of noble living and of wisdom, justice, power, and mercy.

The Interior: Nature, Man, and Society

Although most of the second tour takes one to the interior of the capitol, it begins outside at the sidewalk on the north side, where it anticipates entrance into the

3.9: The main entrance on the north side of the Nebraska State Capitol, showing Alexander's bold statement, "The salvation of the state is watchfulness in the citizen," below the panel of settlers with covered wagon.

3.10: The interior, looking south from the vestibule through the foyer to the rotunda. (Compare figures 2.12 and 2.13.)

The symbolism advances from the concrete to the abstract in two ways: It moves vertically from the floors up the walls to the ceiling in each of the spaces, and at the same time it extends horizontally from the vestibule through the foyer to the rotunda.

We look first at the mosaic designs in the floor. In the vestibule, where the general theme is "Gifts of Nature to Man on the Plains of Nebraska," we find what is essentially a geometric pattern with a cosmic sun symbolized at the center. In Alexander's description, it represents Creation and is the source of other symbols imbedded on other floors.

In accord with this idea, a decorative stem leads from the edge of the vestibule into the foyer, which is dedicated to the theme of "The Life of Man on the Soil of Nebraska." Here Alexander's ideas are developed by three large mosaics: the first represents the foundation provided by the earth, the second plant life, and the third animal life (see figures 5.6, 5.7, and 5.8). These panels are attached symbolically to the large marble mosaic that is the main decorative element in the rotunda, which generally develops the theme "The Virtues of the State" (see figure 5.12).

In his large, circular design for the floor of the rotunda, Alexander again advanced the level of abstraction by representing at its center the earth as the giver of life (see figure 5.11). It is surrounded by four smaller round designs that symbolize animal life and the ancient elements by means of marine forms (Water), reptiles (Fire), birds (Air), and mammals (Earth). Together they represent the progression of four geologic ages; each is encircled by a ribbonlike border decorated with prehistoric animal forms found in Nebraska.

The decorative elements on the walls of the three interior spaces advance the level of abstraction from the basic forms found on the floor. They represent

"The Life of Man on the Soil of Nebraska" in historical sequence, starting again in the vestibule and moving through the foyer to the more highly idealized characterizations found in the rotunda. In the vestibule the dominant designs are murals that were added later; they commemorate the initial occupation of the land by Euroamericans (see figure 6.7). In the foyer the walls are decorated with six murals of more recent design that treat events in the establishment of permanent settlement (see figures 6.8 to 6.13). In the rotunda, three murals commemorate idealized characterizations of the life of man, representing "Labors of the Hand," "Labors of the Heart," and "Labors of the Head" (see figure 6.6).

The ceilings, like the floors, are richly decorated with mosaics, though now at the highest level of abstraction. The focus of the vestibule remains on the natural world (figure 3.11). The symbol of the sun is depicted in the crown of the dome and is accented by representations of the four seasons (see figure 5.2). They, in turn, are surrounded by a frieze of eight panels symbolizing "The First Fruits of the Soil." The whole is circumscribed by the inscription: BEHOLD THEY COME AS HOUSEHOLDERS BRINGING EARTH'S FIRST FRUITS, REJOICING THAT THE SOIL HATH REWARDED THEIR LABORS WITH THE ABUNDANCE OF THE SEASON. The pendentives supporting the dome portray four agricultural activities: plowing, sowing, cultivating, and reaping.

In the foyer, the ceiling again calls attention to "The Life of Man on the Soil of Nebraska." Here the circular mosaics in the crowns of the three bays depict in abstract ways a historical sequence: The first represents "Traditions of the Past," the second "Life of the Present," and the third "Ideals of the Future" (see figure 5.9). Mosaic panels in the arches supporting the

3.11: The richly decorated ceiling of the vestibule.

domes reinforce these symbols with a series of eighteen designs, all of which are highly idealistic.

The symbolism culminates with a decorative and idealistic flourish in the dome of the rotunda (see figure 5.12). Here eight identical winged symbols of the virtues necessary for a civilized society—Temperance, Courage, Justice, Wisdom, Magnaminity, Faith, Hope, and Charity—radiate out from the center of the dome. Done mostly in brilliant blue and gold mosaic tiles, the design has each of the figures holding hands with its neighbors, thereby symbolizing mutual support.

Another important element in Alexander's design for the rotunda is the inscription carved into the frieze below the dome and its pendentives: HE WHO WOULD DULY ENQUIRE ABOUT THE BEST FORM OF THE STATE OUGHT FIRST TO DETERMINE WHICH IS THE MOST ELIGIBLE LIFE / MEN SHOULD NOT THINK IT SLAVERY TO LIVE ACCORDING TO THE RULE OF THE CONSTITUTION FOR IT IS THEIR SALVATION / LAWS AND CONSTITUTIONS SPRING FROM THE MORAL DISPOSITIONS OF THE MEMBERS OF THE STATE / LAW AND ORDER DELIVER THE SOUL / A COMMUNITY LIKE AN INDIVIDUAL HAS A WORK TO DO. Alexander derived these inscriptions from Aristotle's *Politics* and Plato's *Dialogues*. Like the inscriptions mounted above the main entrance to the capitol, these words were chosen by Alexander to remind us in this lofty way of that work which is ours to do.

The Unity of the Plan

By studying both the exterior and interior parts of Alexander's program for the symbols and inscriptions of the capitol, we can appreciate its coherence, its integration with the architecture, and its complex internal relationships. Alexander started with Goodhue's composition, conceiving it as part of the environment. The two tours of the capitol described here progress both horizontally and vertically, intersecting each other at the point of entry (the north portal), which incorporates themes from both. The logical fit of the program to the form of the building is heightened in the complex interweaving of themes evident at the entrance portal and in the symbolic use of the interlude at the south pavilion (see figures 3.1 and 3.6).

Although the major themes and the structure of Alexander's program have been outlined here, the richness evident in its detailed execution has only been suggested. Alexander likened his work to a book that opens to the people of Nebraska a synopsis of the state's history and traditions. One may read this book more carefully than has been possible here and discover individual paragraphs and sentences that further elucidate Alexander's conception. His program was richly developed in minute detail. Although much of it was never executed (for example, the schemes for the Law Library and Memorial Hall), and even though some of the decorative symbolism was determined before Alexander's involvement in the project (such as in the programs for the Governor's Suite, the Supreme Court chambers, and the selection of the Sower as the climactic symbol), the scheme dominates one's impressions of the decorative features of the capitol. Alexander's programs for the Senate and House chambers, which commemorate the Indians and the European settlers, are also worthy of careful contemplation.

A Mature Collaboration

The integration of the arts is evident everywhere in the capitol. It required the mature collaboration of all the artists, not merely that of architect and symbologist. But the addition of Alexander to the team enhanced the quality of the achievement. Goodhue was highly pleased with his collaboration with Alexander; each had won the full confidence of the other. Soon after Goodhue placed Alexander in full charge of the symbological program in September 1923, he asked Alexander to collaborate with him on the plans for the Los Angeles Public Library. Alexander responded quickly with a program that Goodhue considered to be superior even to what he had done for the Nebraska capitol. In some ways Alexander had become to Goodhue what Ralph Adams Cram had been to him before they ended their partnership, that is, the intellectual source for defining meaningful ornament. Tragically, Goodhue died in April 1924, thereby ending a most fruitful collaboration.

Fortunately, Alexander's art as symbologist is not limited to his work on the Nebraska capitol. It may be found on several architectural monuments of renown. In addition to his contribution to the Los Angeles Public Library, he participated in the designs for the Oregon State Capitol, Rockefeller Center in New York City, Joslyn Art Museum in Omaha, Memorial Stadium at the University of Nebraska, and two buildings in the Chicago Century of Progress Exposition in 1933. His work was regarded so highly by members of the American Institute of Architects that that professional organization made him an honorary member.

But it was the Nebraska State Capitol, above all, that allowed Alexander to synthesize his talents and unite his logical and emotional instincts. In this work the classical and the romantic, the humanistic and the spiritual, the philosophic and the poetic were fused in art that transcended local subject matter to attain universality. This building reveals a unique contribution to American culture made by a man who was at once philosopher, educator, anthropologist, and poet.

4 Art, Architecture, and Humanism: The Sculpture of Lee Lawrie

Dale L. Gibbs

An aesthetic miracle occurs when art and architecture work together in harmony to express human ideals. When the arts are united in a single creative achievement, the totality exceeds the sum of its parts taken individually. The finest examples of such a harmony of the arts in the history of Western civilization are the great Gothic cathedrals of Europe. But we seldom see it in contemporary architecture.

Like the Gothic cathedral, the Nebraska State Capitol also represents a harmony of the arts. The sequences of images created by Lee Lawrie, the sculptor who was commissioned to work with Bertram Goodhue, are modeled on concepts or patterns found in Gothic cathedrals. Built in an age when few common people could read or write, the medieval churches transmitted the message of Christianity through sculpture and stained-glass windows. They were at once instructive and inspiring. While the architecture lifts our spirits, filling us with the wonders of infinity, the decorative elements convey at a touchable human level the familiar stories of the Bible, especially the life of Christ.

In the Nebraska capitol the collaboration between Lawrie and Goodhue—between sculptor and architect—exemplifies the definition of art as the interpretation of experience. As the historian and author Jacques Barzun observed, "Art develops, not out of other art, but out of life." In its broadest meaning, art intensifies, clarifies, and interprets human experience.

This definition was made clear to me in a personal way when I was a graduate student in architecture at Yale University. I had been assigned the task of designing a city hall that was to have a grand staircase. My professor, observing my struggle with problems of dimension, placement, proportion, and other details, asked, "Why don't you simply try to design a stairway that breathes with the dignity of man?" His question taught me the difference between architecture and mere building. Unlike the latter, the former always addresses the nature of human aspirations. Although architecture treats the complex relationship of utility with beauty, it rises above the ordinary only when it recognizes and celebrates the nature of man.

It is in this sense that the Nebraska State Capitol embodies the union of art, architecture, and humanism. Here the architectural or formal expression joins with the artistic or symbolic expression to produce a cultural artifact based on a humanistic theme. Humanism in this usage refers not merely to an appreciation of the so-called humanities, but more broadly to attitudes of thought and action based on human values.

The essence of the Nebraska State Capitol is thus the representation of particular human values through art and architecture. Inspired by the physical and cultural context of Nebraska, this building epitomizes the ideals common to the state and the roots from which they developed. It is a convincing and moving evocation of humanistic concern expressed in form, space, and detail. It is a tribute to the exceptional group of artists who created it.

A Harmony of the Arts

The artistic unity of the Nebraska State Capitol is all the more remarkable because its principal designers were in effect outsiders. Lee Lawrie, like Bertram Goodhue, had never seen the Nebraska plains; neither was acquainted with the prairie culture they were commissioned to interpret. Yet the sensitivity and perceptiveness of their interpretation is awesome. Given the considerable quality of their individual talents, one wonders how their creations could exist so harmoniously without diminishing the force of their individual contributions.

What holds the various elements of this design together? What accounts for the magnificent and harmonious interplay between architectural form and the decorative elements? One might attribute the cohesion to the binding force of the architect's original conception. But could it alone account for the integration of the arts that is the hallmark of this building? Goodhue died in 1924, and some elements of his original, dynamic vision were altered after his death.

The answer lies not merely in the clarity of Goodhue's conception, but also in the extraordinary contribution of Hartley Burr Alexander, the philosopher who provided the humanistic and symbolic themes that guided the individual artists. Ever mindful of the architecture, Alexander outlined a thematic program that is rich, comprehensive, and explicit. His decorative scheme for the exterior moves from the historic and concrete at the lower level to the symbolic and abstract on the tower. The interior themes represent nature, life on the prairie, the virtues that sustain society, Plains Indian culture, the coming of the white man, and the historic gifts of the world to the spirit of man.

The task that Alexander outlined for Lee Lawrie was formidable: he was to present through sculpture the spirit of the law as observed in the history of Western civilization. Lawrie responded with art that symbolizes human longing for freedom, justice, and equality, and the conviction that these ideals are best achieved through a system of laws. Any one of his works found in the capitol may not be impressive individually, but collectively they represent clearly the human need to create order out of chaos.

Lee Lawrie, the Sculptor

Lee Lawrie was born in Germany in 1878. At the age of four he emigrated with his parents to the United

4.1: Lee Lawrie, date unknown.

York City. In that instance, Lawrie completed more than sixty figures for the reredos. During his long career (he lived until 1963), he executed many pieces in the traditional Gothic style in which figures are attached to but not fully engaged with the architecture. Thus, when Goodhue asked Lawrie to collaborate with him again in 1921, Lawrie was richly experienced in precisely the kind of architectural sculpture favored by Goodhue, and at the age of forty-three he was at the peak of his artistic powers (figure 4.1).

The Challenge of the Nebraska State Capitol

The design of the Nebraska State Capitol marked a critical turning point in Bertram Goodhue's life as an architect. Before 1919, Goodhue's primary concern was with Gothic architecture. Even though he executed buildings in other derivative styles, notably Spanish Colonial, his reputation was built on his Gothic designs. But with the Nebraska commission, Goodhue made a break with the Gothic Revival and presented a scheme that was essentially classical in its conception. Drawing on Beaux-Arts traditions, he emphasized balance and symmetry, with all elements enclosed within a highly ordered and functional scheme. The general aesthetic and spatial effect is very much in the classical tradition.

States, where he spent the remainder of his life. He lacked formal training in sculpture as a young man, though he later earned a bachelor of fine arts degree from Yale University. In his youth he found employment in a sculpture studio, and during those years he worked with several well-known sculptors, including Augustus Saint-Gaudens. Nevertheless, he was essentially self-taught and he gradually developed a specialization in architectural decoration. In 1900 he began an association with Bertram Goodhue that lasted until the latter's untimely death. Most of Lawrie's early work with Goodhue was on commissions for buildings in the Gothic Revival style, the most famous of which was St. Thomas Episcopal Church in New

Goodhue conceived the formal qualities of this building at a time when the richness of the Beaux-Arts style was being challenged by the cold and impersonal theories of modernism. The creative eclecticism of the Beaux-Arts tradition and the use of historical styles, such as the Gothic, were fading rapidly as the so-called International Style achieved increasing popularity in the 1920s and 1930s. But like most prominent American architects of the time, Goodhue continued to create in terms of the old categories. Thus, even though his Nebraska design may impress us today as wonderfully serene and traditional, he offered a solution that was strikingly original for 1920, a time when popular taste for public architecture continued to be defined by the image created by the national capitol in Washington.

The Nebraska commission offered Lawrie a formidable challenge. Goodhue's architectural massing and formal organization was a new departure from established forms, and the decorative theme developed by Alexander was comprehensive and complex. Both Goodhue and Alexander were highly explicit as to their intentions: Alexander spelled out his theme in great detail and specified which great historical figures and events were to be depicted; Goodhue, even in his earliest sketches, clearly indicated his ideas about the role and function of the sculptural elements.

What did this mean for Lawrie? As an artist who took great pride in his work and who insisted on the highest quality possible, he might have chafed under the explicitness of these directives. Much to his credit, however, he responded with creative energy and added nobility to the decorative theme, thereby reinforcing the brilliance of the architecture.

To appreciate the measure of Lawrie's accomplishment as the sculptor, it is helpful to recall the sequences of images and symbols that Alexander had included in his comprehensive plan for the capitol. He had specified, first, that above the great terrace of the base were to appear a series of eighteen bas-relief panels representing the history of law, beginning with Moses bringing the law from Mount Sinai and ending with Nebraska's admission to the Union.

Second, on the south side of the capitol, Alexander interrupted this series with the south pavilion. Architecturally, the south pavilion is an enormously effective composition; it corresponds in dignity to the great north portal, which is the main entrance to the capitol. The balustrade at the center of the south pavilion, behind which are the chambers of the Supreme Court, includes three panels: "The Signing of the Declaration of Independence," "The Magna Carta," and "The Writing of the Constitution." These three panels are of special interest because they represent the great historical documents that form the basis of our political liberties. Above the bas-reliefs and integrated with the architecture of the south pavilion, Alexander called for images of the great lawgivers of the Western world (figure 4.2).

As a third element in the exterior iconography, Alexander ordered that eight engaged figures be integrated into the base of the tower. Designed as parts of the great transept buttresses and viewed best from the inner courtyards, where the viewer is more closely engaged with the building, these figures were intended by Alexander to "represent the genius of human civilizations," symbols of the ideals of culture that the law defends and nourishes.

Finally, at the top of the golden dome, the plan called for the huge image of the Sower. This monumental figure was to symbolize not only the foundations of life in the soil, but also the idea that the chief purpose of man in forming societies is to sow the seeds for noble living.

Thus, the challenge posed by Alexander's conceptual scheme to Lawrie's skill as a sculptor was daunting. The ideas of some of the panels and some of the figures are readily recognized by persons knowledgeable about our own culture, but others are obscure. Most viewers can easily make the connection between the bas-relief of "The Signing of the Declaration of Independence" with the Supreme Court chambers that lie behind the balustrade of the south pavilion, but few

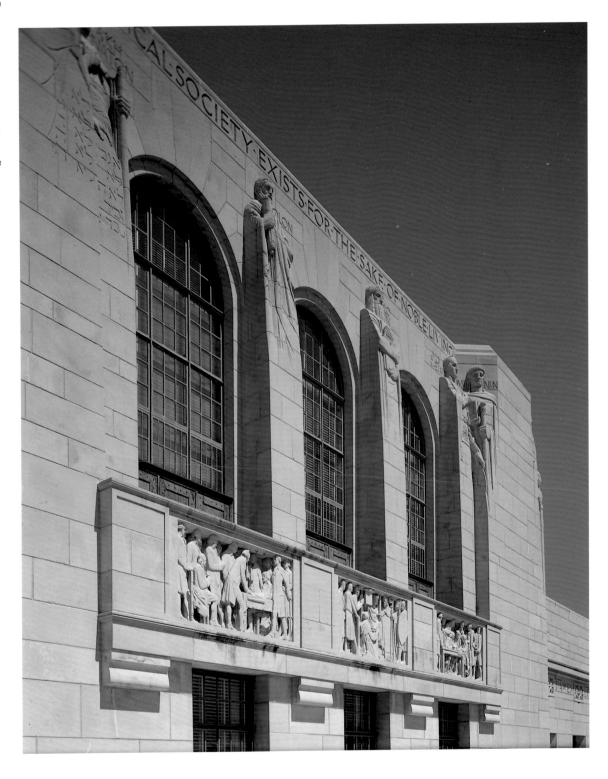

4.2: Lawrie's engaged sculptures, on the south pavilion, of the lawgivers Solon, Solomon, Julius Caesar, and Justinian, above the bas-relief panels of "The Signing of the Declaration of Independence," "The Signing the Magna Carta," and "The Writing the Constitution of the United States."

will make the connection between Napoleon and the Louisiana Purchase, which is the theme of one of the bas-relief panels on the east side of the terrace circuit. We may readily recognize the place of Abraham Lincoln in the spiritual history of our society, but the Egyptian pharaoh Akhnaton as a great lawgiver of the Western world is beyond our ken.

Alexander thus presented Lawrie with a decorative theme that was specific in its sequence; all events and figures were identified. It remained for the artist to execute the work with aesthetic sensibility, remembering always the subordinate relationship of the sculptures to the architectural forms.

Lawrie's Achievement

Lawrie met Alexander's challenge by designing panels and figures that have artistic integrity in their own right, and yet they add to the texture and form of the building without distraction. His bas-relief over the north portal, "The Spirit of the Pioneers," seems in per-

fect balance with the architectural strength of the portal arch. His treatment of the bison at the sides of the north-entry balustrades are models of conventionalized sculpture (figure 4.3). In both cases, one first sees the architectural form, but the eye lingers to absorb the secondary meanings conveyed through the sculpture and inscriptions.

The bas-reliefs on the east and west sides of the terrace circuit presented a problem for Lawrie. According to Alexander's plan they were to depict the history of law in the ancient and modern worlds. Should Lawrie, inspired by Goodhue's exploration of a new architecture, develop new sculptural modes? Or should he follow Alexander's decorative intention for conventional pictorial images? Lawrie decided to remain true to Alexander's plan that the panels were to tell a story and that they should tell it through images that were understandable to the average citizen. His style therefore is crisp but conventional. Like illustrations in a textbook for a high school class in government or political science, the figures and their grouping are familiar. The series has symbolic qualities: the panels offer recognizable images that convey spiritual meanings.

Lawrie's treatment of the great lawgivers on the south pavilion—Minos, Hammurabi, Moses, Akhnaton, Solon, Solomon, Julius Caesar, Justinian, Charlemagne, and Napoleon—reveal his work in its most expressive and impressive form (figure 4.4). Here the sculptor incorporated into the architecture ten heroic figures whose scale and spacing introduce an important change of rhythm and texture in the terrace façade. The style of these figures is idealized and abstract. They are designed to be read clearly but without disrupting the form of the pavilion. In contrast to the figures on the buttresses of the north portal

4.3: Bas-relief panel of bison cow with calf, outside the cheek of the east balustrade, north entrance.

4.4: Lawrie's engaged sculpture of Charlemagne, east side of the south pavilion.

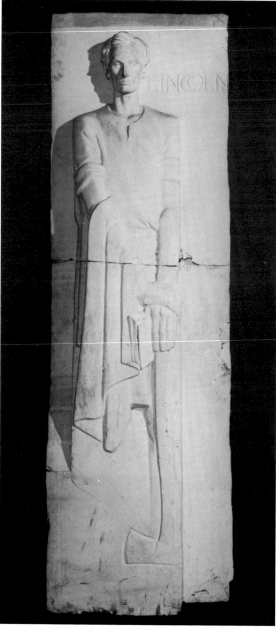

4.5: Lawrie's clay model for King Louis IX of France, who represents "The Age of Chivalry." The completed sculpture is on the east face of the tower, south side.

4.6: Lawrie's clay model for Abraham Lincoln, the Great Emancipator, representing "The Liberation of Peoples." The completed sculpture is on the north face of the tower, east side.

4.7: The Sower, by Lee Lawrie.

(compare figure 3.1), where their effect is weakened by the focus on the main entrance and the grand staircase, the images on the south pavilion are more prominent. They rise dramatically above the double back staircase that connects the terrace with a minor entrance below. The two massive buttresses of the pavilion are joined lightly but surely by the graceful windows of the court chambers and the horizontal tie of the balustrade. In Lawrie's hands this strong architectural composition is complemented, not threat-

But in his treatment of the eight images at the base of the tower, Lawrie found it impossible to follow Alexander's program precisely. Here Alexander had specified that lengthy inscriptions accompany figures that were in several cases to represent types rather than historic persons. For example, "The Dawn of History" was to be symbolized by an Egyptian scribe, "The Age of Chivalry" by a medieval knight, and "The Discovery of Nature" by a Renaissance scientist.

In each case the inscriptions were simply dropped as impractical and historic figures were substituted for the archetypes. Lawrie thus represented history with an obscure Egyptian scribe named Pentaour (see figure 4.5); King Louis IX of France (Saint Louis) was called to duty as the symbol of chivalry (figure 4.5); and Isaac Newton serves as the scientist. They were joined by the Prophet Ezekiel ("Cosmic Tradition"), Socrates ("The Birth of Reason"), Marcus Aurelius ("The Reign of Law"), the Apostle John ("The Glorification of Faith"), and Abraham Lincoln ("The Liberation of Peoples") (figure 4.6). All the figures in this series, like the lawgivers, are architecturally engaged. Each is designed with strong vertical lines with conventionalized decorative elements; the facial expression of each is stern and determined. Collectively these images are excellent examples of Lawrie's skill, though their symbolism is largely lost by their considerable remove from the viewer below.

The most striking and the most famous of Lawrie's sculptures is the Sower, which rests atop the dome, more than four hundred feet above the ground (figure 4.7). This monumental image, nineteen feet tall and weighing more than seven tons, rests on a pedestal designed as a highly stylized sheaf of wheat. Intended to suggest a rugged farmer of the pioneer period, it is more clearly reminiscent of a preindustrial French

ened, by the engaged sculpture. His images of the great lawgivers of the Western world are both strong and conventional. As key elements in the impressive composition of the south elevation, they are the means Lawrie used to convert a challenge into an opportunity.

4.8: Lawrie's clay model for Napoleon in the lawgiver series. In this instance the physical appearance of Lawrie's subject is well known. The completed sculpture is on the south pavilion, east side, facing toward the back.

peasant, for Lawrie adapted his image from a nineteenth-century painting, *The Sower*, by Jean-François Millet. The heavy musculature and faintly archaic style, however, are typical of much public sculpture executed in the 1930s. Although Lawrie's huge statue fails to convey any sense of individuality, it successfully symbolized the historical importance of agriculture for Nebraska.

Perhaps the greatest challenge for Lawrie was to create convincing images of great figures from the past about whose physical appearance we know nothing. It was relatively easy for the sculptor to produce representations of such famous men as Thomas Jefferson (who appears in the panel "The Signing of the Declaration of Independence"), Abraham Lincoln, Napoleon, or even Julius Caesar (figure 4.8). We know what they looked like from paintings and busts done from life. Lawrie was comparatively free to treat these figures abstractly within their architectural context. But the absence of likenesses, as in the cases of Hammurabi, Moses, or Solon, does not give the artist license to improvise freely. He must still create a presence that is credible, one that conforms to our understanding of the man and his accomplishments (figure 4.9).

When a group of such figures is to be created, as Lawrie did with the lawgivers of the Western world in the south pavilion, individual images must follow consistent artistic discipline. The sculptor cannot risk the chance in such a majestic grouping that one figure might depart noticeably from the pattern; at the same time, the sculptor must somehow project a presence strong enough to carry us beyond the image to the idea. Lawrie could draw upon his broad understanding of the history of sculpture to create suggestive images, but he needed to go beyond that to project his

4.9: Lawrie's interpretation of Hammurabi in the series of law-givers, on the south pavilion, west side.

4.10: Lawrie' clay model for "Wisdom and Justice," on the left pylon of the north entrance. (Compare figure 3.1.)

understanding of the place of these men in history. Through his images, Lawrie had to convey the greatness of their ideas and their contributions to civilization. This is not a task for amateurs. It is even beyond the powers of a gifted sculptor if he is incapable of sublimating his individuality to a grand scheme.

In this respect Lawrie succeeded on a grand scale. Both the lawgivers of the south pavilion and the great heroes of Western civilization at the base of the tower reveal subtle abstraction. The chiseled planes of the figures catch the light with a grace that leaves them intimately engaged with the architecture and yet effectively registers their essential individuality.

In addition to problems of sensibility and projection, Lawrie had to overcome technical difficulties. The sculptures were carved in place from great chunks of Indiana limestone; skilled craftsmen had to transfer the measurements of the figures from clay or plaster models, called maquettes, to the blocks of stone (see figures 4.5 and 4.6). The maquettes were constructed in Lawrie's studio in New York and shipped to Lincoln. This meant that Lawrie had to account for the intensity and direction of light, distances from the viewer, and the position of a given figure in relation to other elements of the design—all under artificial conditions. Nevertheless, as the sculptor Lawrie remained solely responsible for the creation of the figures, even though the actual carving of the stone was done by others in Lincoln.

This is not to suggest that Lawrie was unfamiliar with conditions in Lincoln. He made frequent trips to Nebraska to direct the progress of the work. He confided to his wife that he had "some of the best stone carvers in the world" working on the project. The quality of this workmanship was consistently excellent. It included not only the engaged figures and the de-

tailed panels, but also the eclectic capitals on interior columns, the great wooden doors to the legislative chambers, and even the delicate birds that Lawrie included as parts of his design for the balustrade surrounding the rotunda. One senses that it was a labor of love and dedication, inspired by a magnificent architectural concept and infused with the energy of a noble vision.

Criticisms of Lawrie's Work

Taken as a whole, Lawrie's work on the Nebraska State Capitol is a major achievement in American art. In some respects it is sublime. Still, the scale and complexity of the project were such that certain artistic problems were virtually inescapable.

For example, although his technique of faceted abstraction was highly effective in his execution of male figures, it was less successful with the female figures on the north portico, where his projection of Wisdom and Mercy produced rather androgenous images (figure 4.10). The architectural composition required that the female figures be the same height as the male. The female Wisdom is paired with the male Justice on the left; they are balanced on the right with the male Power and female Mercy. The result is that Wisdom and Mercy seem Amazonian. Moreover, Lawrie had to express both male and female characteristics through similar draperies, headdresses, and applied symbols. This resulted in an overly active composition: the two side pylons seem to impinge upon the authority of the central portico with its great rounded arch. Thus, Lawrie's technique, which is so evocative in his treatment of such single figures as Napoleon or Minos, produces images that seem bland and unmoving in the pairs.

The bas-relief panels are also of an uneven quality. For example, the three panels of the south pavilion, which illustrate the signing of the Magna Carta, the Declaration of Independence, and the United States Constitution, are stately yet relaxed compositions (figure 4.11). In contrast, the panel on the south side of the southwestern corner at the terrace level, which depicts "The Codification of Roman Law under Justinian," offers a dull grouping of figures, all in profile with stiff, stylized garments (figure 4.12). Similarly, the treatment of "The Codification of Anglo-Saxon Law under Ethelbert" uses a flat, primitive style, probably to suggest the ancient, almost mythical, character of the event (figure 4.13). In general, Lawrie chose to execute the bas-reliefs of the terrace circuit in different artistic styles related to time and subject: Assyrian, Roman, Greek, and simplified naturalism. Nevertheless, his work is the most evocative and appealing in the naturalist style, and less confident and elegant in the archaic styles.

Some of Lawrie's critics have found his figurative sculptures to be monotonous and rigid, having a lifeless or mannequin character. It is true that under certain conditions, such as the gray days of winter, figures that sparkle in bright sunlight can almost fade into the gray mass of the building. Still, it may be beyond the power of any sculptor of bas-relief panels to transcend the deadening effect of dreary weather.

Most critics, however, have admired Lawrie's work. At the time of the completion of the capitol in 1932, Lawrie held a secure place in the world of American art. His colleague Adolph Block observed that "his collaboration with Bertram Goodhue produced such a harmonious blend of sculpture and architecture that it has become a goal often sought but seldom achieved by the designers of great edifices of church and state."

But there were dissenters, and they were usually advocates of modernism in architecture. By 1932 the use of historical styles and creative eclecticism was waning. In that year the Museum of Modern Art in New York staged an exhibition celebrating the new International Style as it had developed in the preceding decade—the same years in which the Nebraska State Capitol was built. The curator of that exhibition was a brilliant young architect named Philip Johnson, who, in the years that followed, became one of the most successful advocates and practitioners of modern architecture in the world.

In the catalog of the exhibition Johnson vigorously attacked the very notion of collaboration among artists in architecture. He wrote, "Sculpture also ought not to be combined with or merged with architecture. It should retain its own character quite separately from its background so that the sculpture and the wall are not confused. Contemporary architecture serves as an admirable background for sculpture not specifically designed for that location." Although Johnson probably did not have the Nebraska capitol in mind, his proscription struck at the heart of what Goodhue, Alexander, Lawrie, and the other artists had tried so valiantly and successfully to achieve.

Today Johnson's criticism has a hollow ring. In recent years he himself has abandoned the principle of separation as he has imposed historic styles on modern structures in New York and elsewhere, including one derived from Chippendale furniture. Nevertheless, the view Johnson articulated in 1932 characterized the emerging modern style. It was to be free of historical references, and if sculpture was to be used at all, it was to stand free of its architectural surroundings.

For the next thirty years American architecture was dominated by sleek curtain walls and monotonous façades occasionally punctuated by a free-standing

4.11: "The Constitution of the United States," south pavilion, right panel. (Compare figure 4.2.)

4.12: "The Codification of Roman Law under Justinian," on the terrace circuit, south side, southwestern corner.

4.13: "The Codification of Anglo-Saxon Law under Ethelbert," on the south side, southeastern corner.

sculpture, preferably by Alexander Calder or Isamu Naguchi, with architecture as background. During these decades critics treated the Nebraska State Capitol with kindly indulgence. It was a fine building, they observed, that revealed the last vestiges of Beaux-Arts historicism. Goodhue's conception, which seemed so fresh and innovative in 1919, was dismissed as archaic in a world of steel and glass buildings that reflected, not our cultural heritage, but only each other.

Lawrie's Later Years

In 1940, Lawrie left New York and went to live in Easton, Maryland, on the eastern shore of Chesapeake Bay. At that time he felt that his life as an artist was over, that his work and the architecture it complemented had been replaced by a new sensibility. Fortunately, he misread the signs of the times. He went on receiving commissions to the end of his life.

Lawrie received honors as well. In 1922 he had received the gold medal of the American Institute of Architects for his work on St. Thomas Episcopal Church in New York. This honor was repeated in 1928 for his contribution to the Nebraska State Capitol, considered by most critics to be the crowning achievement of his career. Never debilitated by old age, he continued to work steadily until a week before his death in 1963 at the age of eighty-six.

During the years that followed his Nebraska achievement, Lawrie's reputation suffered not so much from criticism as from neglect. His wonderful maquettes, which were given to the University of Ne-braska, were on one occasion in the 1930s nearly destroyed. They were saved at the last minute by Linus Burr Smith, chairman of the Department of Architecture, who understood their value.

Humanism in Architecture

Beaux-Arts architecture, from which the Nebraska State Capitol derives, was excessively preoccupied with the past, but modernism, with its antihistorical stance, inevitably became the aesthetic of disinheritance. We have lived through decades in which we rejected the past without forming a clear definition of the future. Current trends in architecture reveal a revival of interest in the uses of history, especially in the humanistic ideals and values that enable us to appreciate the nourishing symbols of our culture and to manifest them through art.

The Nebraska State Capitol is not so much an architectural essay on the state as it is a paean to human experience. Here art and architecture exist in a state of harmonious mutuality, each depending on the other to express fully the concept, as Alexander expressed it, of "noble living." Like the Gothic cathedral, this structure embodies a similar harmony in which form, space, and art work together to express purpose and cultural content. As I pass by the capitol and see Lawrie's Sower perched so delicately atop the tower, I am reminded of Henry Adams's closing lines from *Mont-Saint-Michel and Chartres*: "The delight of its aspirations is flung up to the sky. The pathos of its self-distrust and anguish of doubt is buried in the earth as its last secret."

5

The Decorative Art of Hildreth Meiere

Joan Woodside and Betsy Gabb

When Bertram Grosvenor Goodhue and his fellow artists began their great collaboration in the early 1920s, the decorative arts still flourished and their role to enhance, augment, or enrich architecture was unchallenged. In those days, when the modern or International style in architecture was in its infancy, it was taken for granted that decoration was to be an integral part of the whole. Such ideas, which were embedded in Beaux-Arts theory, continued to dominate much architectural thought and practice, as well as public taste, throughout the decade. Goodhue accordingly assumed that his great monument of public architecture, the Nebraska State Capitol, would be graced with mosaics and other forms of decorative art, even though Beaux-Arts architecture was often ornamentally ponderous and sometimes weakened by spatial confusion.

By the 1930s, however, the decade in which the capitol was completed, the functionalist dictum of Ludwig Mies van der Rohe that "less is more" had attracted widespread support. Applied ornament was soon banished; the word *decorative* itself took on connotations of tastelessness and vulgarity. The study of iconography was discarded as irrelevant in the modern age. Only in retrospect do we, living in an era that rejects the chilly formalism of the International Style, recognize that Goodhue used the past as a springboard to the present and future, that he created a truly functional building which defied many of the conventions of his day, and that his conception of monumental public architecture was protomodernist just as ours is postmodernist.

In Goodhue's view, decoration was functional. According to Hartley Burr Alexander, his chief collaborator, Goodhue insisted that "every element of decoration be significant, that there should be interlaced no ornament that is not relevant to the use and meaning of the building." In the hands of a skilled artist, mosaics and other decorative elements could function to invest a public building with cultural significance and social relevance. Goodhue believed that by looking both backward and forward in time he could understand the subtle link between symbolized ideas and their expression in concrete form. Thus, the artist who could produce appropriate mosaic designs for the floors, ceilings, arches, and pendentives of the new capitol would add a rich and textured voice to the harmony of the arts. The person whom Goodhue chose for this imposing task was Hildreth Meiere.

Hildreth Meiere

Meiere, born in New York in 1892, was well trained in art. She was educated in private schools in New York and in 1911 went to Europe, where she studied in Florence, Italy. She subsequently returned to the United States for additional work at the California School of Fine Arts and in New York at the Art Students League and for three years at the Beaux-Arts Institute of Design. By the time she was thirty years old, she had turned almost exclusively to mural decoration in association with architects. It was in this context that her work came to the attention of Goodhue, for whom she decorated the rotunda of the National Academy of Sciences building in Washington, D.C. When Goodhue received the commission to design the Nebraska State Capitol, he made her a member of his team of artists and asked her to produce the mosaics for the domed vestibule of the capitol. This success led, after Goodhue's death, to her major work in the foyer, rotunda, and legislative chambers.

Meiere's understanding of the decorative arts was entirely congruent with Goodhue's. Sensitive to the criticism of the "extreme Left Wing Modernists," as she called those architects who dismissed decoration as the negation of efficiency, Meiere argued in 1932 that "man's impulse toward the decoration of all that touches his life, all that he wears, uses, and lives in, is so universal that it seems that it can be accepted as a fundamental part of human nature."

She also took care to distinguish decoration from ornament. In her view, "decoration is that which gives color or texture, scale or pattern or interest." In choosing a certain brick for a wall, she observed, an architect chooses decoration, but "to design a terrazzo floor is to start ornamenting." She charged that the modernists confused decoration with historic ornament and predicted that eventually they would abandon their attitude. "Human nature demands interest and relief from barrenness by some sort of enrichment," she wrote; the human instinct to decorate is "insuppressible."

Meiere's Nebraska work was so successful that she was awarded the gold medal of the Architectural League in 1928. By the end of the decade she had earned a reputation as one of the finest decorators in the United States and soon became head of the mural-painting department in the Beaux-Arts Institute of Design in New York, where she had once been a student. Her career was long and fruitful. Several years before her death in 1961, she wrote happily but without arrogance: "Having begun at the top with the National Academy of Sciences and the Nebraska State Capitol, the long list of commissions, well over a hundred, have come of themselves."

The Mosaics of the Vestibule

Accustomed to working with architects, Meiere understood that her designs had to conform to the specifications outlined by Hartley Burr Alexander in his sym-

bolic program for interior decorations and inscriptions. Alexander chose the subject matter; she was to give his ideas concrete form in mosaics.

The theme chosen by Alexander for the vestibule was "Gifts of Nature to Man on the Plains of Nebraska." For a person entering the capitol through the main entrance on the north side, this interior space offers a dramatic contrast to the bland stone exterior. Like the early Christian churches of the fifth and sixth centuries, the vestibule produces an experience of wonder. The upward sweep of the soaring interior provides ample space for brilliant mosaics in reds, browns, blues, and gold (see figure 3.11).

The floor is dominated by a huge stylized sun that symbolizes Creation and consists of pieces of green, brown, tan, black, gray, and white marble (figure 5.1). The entire composition, which includes smaller surrounding celestial forms, symbolizes the sun as the source of energy. It establishes the decorative pattern for the several tondi (circular or medallion forms) that progress majestically from the vestibule through the foyer to the rotunda.

5.2: Meiere's design for the dome of the vestibule. A stylized sun is at the center, surrounded by symbols of the seasons, the signs of the zodiac, and representations of the first fruits of the soil.

5.3: The dome of the baptistry, Cathedral of Ravenna (sixth century), Italy. Meiere's design for the dome of the vestibule apparently drew its inspiration from this Italian model.

four rectangular panels, each of which portrays a personification of one of the four seasons; each figure is dressed in an ancient costume appropriate to the season represented. Together the sun and the four panels form a Greek cross.

Occupying the spaces between the arms of the cross are four squares depicting seasonally appropriate signs of the zodiac. The lower concentric section of the vestibule dome design is composed of eight panels in ceramic tile mosaics that symbolize "The First Fruits of the Soil" in Nebraska: cattle, wheat, flowers, swine, grass (hay), fruits, sheep, and corn.

Between the panels depicting the gifts of Nature are elongated rectangular mosaics that depict altars and temples. Here Meiere drew upon her familiarity with Italian forms. These insertions are based upon similar images placed at the rim of the dome in the cathedral baptistry in Ravenna, Italy, a city known for its brilliant Byzantine mosaics (figure 5.3). Meiere's inclusion of altars and temples may have been intended to suggest that the Nebraska capitol is a temple that houses the body and spirit of the law.

The style Meiere employed for the mosaics in the dome is reminiscent of surviving panels from the fourth-century Basilica of Junius Bassius in Rome. The figures in those mosaics are of a short or stumpy variety associated with Roman plebian art rather than the patrician. The panels were executed in a technique called *opus sectile*. Instead of using the refined square pieces (tesserae) that are traditionally used in mosaics, this technique calls for jagged, irregular chunks of marble, stone, ceramic, or glass to be laid in grout to form the desired shapes. The use of the larger, irregular pieces creates both greater variety and a more primitive and powerful impression. Meiere adapted this style in all of the panels in the vestibule

High above the symbolic sun on the vestibule floor is another in the center of the dome (figure 5.2). Like its counterpart on the floor, it radiates light, heat, and energy—the first of Nature's gifts to man. Extending out from the circular form of the sun in the dome are

dome, as well as in the four designs placed on the supporting pendentives, where four activities of agriculture—plowing, sowing, cultivating, and reaping—are symbolized. Although marble and stone traditionally were used in such panels, Meiere effectively caught the primitive spirit of the *opus sectile* technique by using ceramic tiles, an innovation favored by Goodhue. The colors are strong; brilliant blues dominate red, brown, and white.

The Mosaics on the Floor of the Foyer

According to Hartley Burr Alexander, who planned the symbology of the entire capitol, the designs of the foyer are not those first approved by Goodhue. It happened by chance in 1925 that he and Hildreth Meiere met in Italy, and together they studied the art of the great cathedrals in the Tuscan hill country. Inspired by the magnificent floor mosaics in the Cathedral of Siena, they resolved to draw up a new plan, which they

later did in Paris. Upon their return to the United States, they received the enthusiastic approval of the architects and the Capitol Commission to proceed.

The ideas that Meiere developed in creating the designs of the capitol floor thus were directly inspired by the Sienese model, including designs and techniques drawn from the *pavimento* (pavement) in the cathedral. Although many panels in the varicolored marble floor at Siena were executed in traditional inlay, others were done in the sgraffito, or scratch, technique, which employs gently incised lines to create shapes and forms.

Meiere's floor mosaics are also reminiscent of simplified line drawings found on Greek vases. Her figures, however, have a streamlined shape or flowing movement suggestive of the Art Deco style that was popular in the 1930s. For the pictorial panels, she used only two marbles, light and dark, which she chose for their capacity to sharpen contrasts and en-

5.4: This mosaic design for the floor leading from the vestibule into the foyer symbolizes "The Genius of Creative Energy."

5.5: The floor designs of the foyer, showing the relationships of the three large tondi. The view is from the north, looking south toward the rotunda.

rich the surface. For the designs that frame her pictures, she selected a limited palette of mostly grays and greens.

The first design, situated at the entrance to the foyer, symbolizes the personification of cosmic energy (figure 5.4). A male nude, patterned on ancient descriptions of Zeus and other Olympian gods, rides dramatically through space, shaping stars and suns. In his right hand he holds a lightning bolt; his left hand gathers the reins controlling an unseen chariot that is symbolic of cosmic forces—not only the sun and other celestial bodies, but also the wind, water, heat, and lightning.

This panel is a logical extension of the sun symbolism of the vestibule and provides a transition to the tripartite foyer, where three large tondi dominate the floor designs (figure 5.5). Each is enclosed in a square bordered with much patterned ornament. The first, or

northernmost, tondo presents a long-haired female figure pushing against rocks on either side. Identified by Alexander as the Divider of the Rocks, she represents the foundation of the earth and symbolizes the mineral world (figure 5.6).

The second tondo, which occupies the center space of the foyer floor, is "The Spirit of Vegetation" (figure 5.7). It offers a representation of Flora, the Roman goddess of flowers, done in a style reminiscent of Sandro Botticelli, a great painter of the Italian Renaissance. In his famous painting *Primavera*, Botticelli drew his inspiration from the Roman poet Ovid. As Ovid told the story, Chloris, the Greek goddess of flowers, had fled from the wind Zephyr. Botticelli depicted the moment when Zephyr caught Chloris and embraced her. As flowers fell from her lips, she was transformed into the Roman goddess Flora. Meiere's image of Flora offers a parallel to Botticelli's and a hint of his style. Her rendition has the goddess seated gracefully in a grove of trees. Blooming flowers grow in front of her, mushrooms to her left. She touches the mushrooms lightly, thereby symbolizing the calling forth of plant life.

In the third tondo an older female figure representing Fauna touches the chin of a lioness with one hand as she strokes its haunch with the other (figure 5.8). Symbolizing "The Spirit of Animal Life," she appears as the guardian of animals. She is joined by a goat and a monkey—or, more properly, an ape—which in classical iconography is the symbol of art.

The final design of the foyer floor, located at the threshold of the rotunda, is a rectangular panel that features a large male figure with the wings of an eagle. He wears a wreath of victory. Characterized by Alexander as an Eros figure, he gently releases floral and faunal seed: pine cones with his left hand and insects

5.6: The first, or northernmost, tondo of the foyer floor mosaics, entitled ''The Spirit of the Soil.'' It has also been called ''The Divider of the Rocks.'' In either case, the design is symbolic of the foundation for life provided by the structural earth.

5.7: ''The Spirit of Vegetation,'' the central tondo of the foyer floor.

5.8: ''The Spirit of Animal Life,'' the third tondo of the foyer floor.

hooded figure, symbolizing "Traditions of the Past," who is writing the history of the state. The center design, "Life of the Present," shows two figures: a mother and her son. The woman pulls a heavy thread, symbolic of the passage of time, from a distaff (an instrument used to hold flax or wool in spinning). The third figure is also hooded. Representing "Ideals of the Future," it touches a crystal ball with its left hand (figure 5.9). Characterized by Alexander as sibyls (women of antiquity with prophetic powers), the figures are therefore female, despite their heavy musculature. In form, style, and color, these figures continue the pattern established in the vestibule dome.

It is likely that Meiere and Alexander drew their inspiration for the ceiling figures from the Cathedral of Siena, where ten sibyls are depicted on the floor of side aisles. However, Meiere did not in this instance follow the Sienese models, which are Early Renaissance. Instead, her figures recall the monumental style used in the High Renaissance by Michelangelo in his portrayal of hooded sibyls on the ceiling of the Sistine Chapel in the Vatican.

The Rotunda Floor

The historical themes developed on the foyer floor serve as the introduction to the more abstract concepts treated in the rotunda, where the theme is "The Virtues of the State." Alexander had prescribed that the floor should represent the Ancient Earth, the foundation of life in Nebraska. Mother Earth was to appear at the center, surrounded by symbols of the four elements of classical antiquity: Earth, Air, Fire, and Water.

Meiere executed this prescription by designing a majestic, enthroned Mother Nature who occupies the center of the rotunda floor (figure 5.10). On her left is a female figure representing agriculture; on the right a

5.9: The ornate ceiling of the foyer with its three medallions symbolizing the past, present, and future.

5.10: Meiere's design for the floor of the rotunda, with the central position occupied by Mother Nature, symbolizing the earth as lifegiver.

with his right. Together, the five panels of the foyer floor symbolize the natural foundation of human life and the successive steps in creation.

The Foyer Ceiling

High above the floor of the cathedrallike space created by the foyer are three mosaic medallions that echo the shapes of the tondi below. The first depicts a

woman pours water from a jar. Before her is a nude boy; in the foreground are baskets overflowing with fruit. The composition is surrounded by a highly conventionalized sun, the source of power and life. Encircling this design is a giant guilloche (an intertwining ornamental band) that encompasses four smaller circles, one for each of the four elements.

The theme of the four elements descends from classical antiquity, when Air, Earth, Fire, and Water were often symbolized by female figures; in the Renaissance they came to be associated with various gods and goddesses. In Meiere's treatment of the theme, they are translated into male figures called genii (quasi-mythological figures intended to personify something immaterial, such as a virtue, custom, or institution). Above Mother Nature appears the Genius of

The guilloche then winds around Fire with a parade of reptiles, including dinosaurs, from the Mesozoic era. The Genius of Air is surrounded by flying reptiles and birds representative of early Tertiary creatures. Finally, a procession of great mammals—mammoths, mastodons, and the like—encircle the Genius of Earth.

The large pattern created by the five tondi and the serpentine guilloche is also derivative of the Cathedral of Siena, where the same design is used in the second panel on the floor of the nave (figure 5.11). Here a plain or undecorated guilloche circles the large central tondo (which depicts "The She-Wolf of Siena") by winding around eight smaller surrounding circles (which bear the symbols of cities allied with Siena). Meiere's design in the Nebraska capitol uses exactly the same pattern, except that Alexander's symbolism allowed only four satellite tondi instead of eight, as in Siena.

5.11: Hildreth Meiere based her design for the rotunda floor on this mosaic in the Cathedral of Siena, Italy. The city of Siena is symbolized at the center of the design; the serpentine guilloche represents its ties to surrounding satellite or allied communities.

5.12: "The Virtues of the State," Meiere's mosaic design for the dome of the rotunda.

Air; accompanied by birds in flight, he rests on a cloud, his long hair streaming in the wind behind him. To the right is the Genius of Earth, a powerful figure hammering away at a rock. The Genius of Fire, surrounded by flames, appears on the left. Below Mother Earth is the Genius of Water, a powerful but gentle figure who holds a large fish. He is submerged, and his hair swirls about as another fish swims close by. All the figures are executed in white marble mosaics set against black.

The guilloche itself, in accordance with Alexander's directive, presents a succession of creatures from the geological history of Nebraska as it winds around the tondi of Mother Nature and the four elements. The series begins with figures from the Paleozoic era. Representative of marine fossils found in the southeastern part of the state, they surround the Genius of Water.

The Rotunda Dome

In Alexander's scheme, the rotunda dome provides the space for the culminating or climactic design of his symbology (figure 5.12). Following his directives, Meiere designed eight winged virtues—Charity, Hope, Courage, Temperance, Wisdom, Faith, Justice, and Magnanimity—who join hands to uphold the state. Each is fundamental for a civilized society to survive; each is like a fluted column or a pillar: strong, straight, and powerful; and each is helmeted, as if joining in a war against vice. Soaring more than a hundred feet above the rotunda floor, these winged geniuses or angels, all equal in shape and importance, form what Alexander called a celestial rose.

Like the ceiling in the vestibule, the dome of the rotunda is similar in style and meaning to that of the cathedral baptistry in Ravenna (see figure 5.3). In that

structure the central portion of the dome depicts large, lively figures of the twelve apostles, each holding a heavenly crown of glory. Their heads are framed by a circle of swag and jabot drapery that surrounds a central medallion. Meiere seems to have translated this motif into the pattern formed by the clasped hands of the virtues.

Although Meiere's design would not be characterized as based on the classic patterns of antiquity, it alludes to classicism in its treatment of the bodies of the eight virtues, which resemble the fluted shafts of classic columns. In other respects, however, they resemble Byzantine linearity more than they recall the Roman realism revealed in the figures in the dome of the Ravenna baptistry.

At a more profound level, however, the two domes are similar. Both extol the importance of living under the rule of law, be it spiritual as in Ravenna, or earthly as in the Nebraska rotunda. In this sense, the Italian structure provided an iconography suitable for translation into forms appropriate for Nebraska.

Meiere's Contribution

Hildreth Meiere's contributions to the artistic harmony of the Nebraska State Capitol extend beyond her work in the vestibule, foyer, and rotunda. Her mosaics in the dome of the old Senate Chamber, for example, are brilliant examples of decorative art. But all of her work demonstrates that she was in complete agreement with Goodhue's principle that decoration be functional in the sense that it should endow the building with historical or cultural significance. Both Goodhue and the symbologist, Hartley Burr Alexander, sought to relate Nebraska to the history of Western civilization. By drawing on ancient, classical, and Renaissance sources, Meiere greatly enhanced their achievement.

6

Unlike other artistic elements of the Nebraska State Capitol, the many paintings that decorate wall spaces in various parts of the building lack stylistic unity. The murals conform generally to the iconography developed by Hartley Burr Alexander, but the fact remains that they were designed and executed by eight artists over a period of four decades. Inevitably they reflect changes in style, technique, and taste. Even though certain unifying conceptions can be identified among them, the casual observer is likely to be impressed more by their artistic differences than their similarities. They remind us of the changes that are often evident in the medieval cathedrals of Europe, which often required centuries to reach completion.

In the United States, the use of murals as interior decorative elements in public buildings developed in the post–Civil War era, when American architects, inspired by French and English examples, introduced their use. Although murals are found in the national capitol in Washington, the tradition had to await full development until the Gothic Revival and Beaux-Arts architectural styles gained popularity in the latter half of the nineteenth century. Among the pioneers in the American school of mural painting were John La Farge and William Morris Hunt.

The Columbian Exposition, held in Chicago in 1893, was the turning point in the development of American mural painting. The temporary buildings of this world's fair provided magnificent spaces in which novice American muralists could develop their skills. Working under the general supervision of Francis Millet, such experienced easel painters as Mary Cassatt, Edward Blashfield, Kenyon Cox, and J. Alden Weir designed murals for the Chicago fair. In general, their work received both professional and popular approval and successfully launched the art of architectural decoration in the United States.

6.1: Augustus Vincent Tack's design for the west wall of the reception room in the governor's suite. The state as protector of the sick and helpless is symbolized on the left; on the right, philosophy, science, and art represent the educational role of the state.

The Governor's Suite: Augustus Vincent Tack, 1927

Among the next generation of muralists was Augustus Vincent Tack (1870–1949), who had studied with La Farge. He was the first artist commissioned to prepare murals for the Nebraska State Capitol, then under construction. One of the first parts of the building to be completed was the Governor's Suite, located on the northeastern side of the main floor. Tack's designs for the governor's office and reception room were installed in 1927, five years before the completion of the building as a whole.

Although Tack is remembered today chiefly for his nonobjective paintings, which recent critics have identified as harbingers of the abstract expressionist style, he was recognized during his lifetime as a painter of portraits and religious subjects in a quasi-Impression-

tury when Mantegna and the Bellini brothers discovered a way to circumvent the problems associated with fresco painting. Exterior dampness that penetrates the wall often causes frescoes to flake and the plaster that supports them to crumble. The Italian masters found that wall paintings on canvas would not only escape the moisture problem but would also be much easier to execute. Upon its completion in a studio, a painting merely had to be glued in place with a compound of white lead and varnish that serves as a moisture barrier between the wall and the painted canvas. This is the technique Tack used for his Nebraska murals.

The suite of rooms designed for the use of the governor, like the other public spaces in the capitol, were included in Alexander's grand iconographic scheme. He designated the barrel-vaulted reception room as the place to expand upon the state's motto, "Equality before the Law," which is inscribed high on the chimney breast above the fireplace on the west wall (figure 6.1). Below this inscription Tack introduced the head of a woman in profile set in a wreath. She represents the pioneer mother, whose work, devotion, and sacrifice made possible present prosperity, which is symbolized by the wreath.

The motto and medallion introduce the viewer to Tack's program for the rest of the room, which begins with three figures in blue on the east wall opposite the fireplace (figure 6.2). They represent Understanding, Justice, and Mercy. Justice is at the center; her hands are steadied by Understanding and Mercy, thereby symbolizing their moderating role in the rule of law. Flanking the central group are representations of citizens of various categories: rich and poor, young and old, strong and weak, young lovers, the family, and motherhood. Above them are eight figures symboliz-

6.2: East wall of the reception room, governor's suite. Symbolic figures of understanding, justice, and mercy occupy the center of Tack's mural. Above them are figures representing civilizations from which American law and culture derive.

istic style. His murals, however, were executed in a manner reminiscent of late Gothic paintings in which modeled figures are placed on a flat, solid-color abstract background.

Tack painted his murals in oils on canvas in his New York studio. He then sent them to Lincoln, where he personally supervised their installation. This technique was not new; it had been in use since the fifteenth cen-

rights of free speech, religious freedom, and universal suffrage. At the left, freedom of speech is symbolized by a group of men whose feet point in different directions, thereby suggesting that democracies tolerate diversity of thought and speech without molestation by law. Religious freedom is represented by a group of five figures. A black-robed male figure at the center signifies the voice of conscience; he is surrounded by four worshipers. Diversity in religious belief is emphasized by an inscription that arcs above the group: "The voice of God is as the sound of many waters." The third grouping honors the right of suffrage (figure 6.3). Several figures, both male and female, line up to cast their ballots into a box held by a woman who, in order to maintain the secrecy of free political choice, averts her eyes from the voter and his ballot.

The institutions of the state are represented on either side of the fireplace on the west wall. On the left, charitable institutions are symbolized by three persons helping an injured or sick person and by a female figure protecting three children, presumably orphans. On the right, state educational institutions are suggested by a youth who extends his hands to symbols of philosophy, science, and art, which are bound together by a ribbon—the unity of knowledge (see figure 6.1). On the north wall, the spaces between the windows are filled by depictions of marriage and motherhood.

Tack's murals in the governor's private office also call for description. Here, in the flat dome above the governor's desk, Tack painted four maidens as symbols of the seasons (figure 6.4). Below the dome in the lunettes between the pendentives are four seasonal murals depicting the plowing of the soil, the cultivation of crops, the harvest, and finally the winter river god and the rewards of the harvest (figure 6.5).

ing past civilizations, all of which are noted for their lawgivers: India, Babylon, Judea, Egypt, Greece, Rome, France (Gallia), and England (Anglia). Together they represent the accumulated legal wisdom of the world. Above them is an inscription taken from the Declaration of Independence: "All men are endowed by their Creator with certain inalienable rights; among these are life, liberty, and the pursuit of happiness."

The south wall of the reception room celebrates the

6.3: "Rights of Suffrage," by Augustus Tack, on the south wall, reception room, Governor's Suite.

6.4: Augustus Tack's decorations in the dome above the governor's desk, including the women representing the four seasons; each of the seasons is symbolized in the lunettes formed by the pendentives.

of the mural figures emphasize the unchanging truth of the message. Tack's use of grayed colors and the simple lines of his designs emphasize the plainness of the chief executive's tasks and separates them from the luxurious furnishings and red silk damask wall hangings that surround the murals. Tack thereby used contrast to accentuate the fact that simple agricultural labor provides present and future wealth.

Tack handled the entire program of murals for the Governor's Suite with a spare style worthy of the Gothic painters he admired. Each topic is treated individually; each of the figure groups occupies a separate wall space, and no attempt is made to tie them together. Instead, unity is achieved through the repetition of colors, a uniform rendering of the figures, and the solid gray background color. Tack's treatment is consistent with the canons of medieval mural decoration that recognize the existence of the wall and respect its value as a structural element. All is flat; not even the slightly rounded figures violate this quality. Still, in a peculiar way, the mural is seen apart from the wall that supports it, for by its very existence it modifies the wall plane. The viewer is thus more conscious of the painting than of the supporting wall. Nevertheless, the two maintain a symbiotic relationship: like a well-fitted piece of clothing, the mural enhances the architectural body that gives it form. It lends vibrancy to the space and emphasizes architectural relationships, thereby intensifying the viewer's sense of standing in a particular space, even as the painting tells a story or teaches a lesson.

6.5: Augustus Tack's mural of the harvest, governor's private office.

6.6: "The Spirit of the Prairie," by Elizabeth Dolan, on the north wall of the Law Library.

The program devised by Alexander for the Governor's Suite is highly didactic. He intended to instruct the governor in certain facts about the administration of this high office. It is not by chance that Justice is flanked by Mercy and Understanding; each time the governor passes through the reception room into the private office beyond, the chief executive is reminded of the duties that attend this branch of state government. Portraits of Benjamin Franklin and Abraham Lincoln are also present in the reception room and provide models of statesmanship for the governor's contemplation. In the governor's private office, paintings of the four seasons emphasize the fact that agriculture, which is dependent upon seasonal changes, is central to the Nebraska's economy. Above the governor's desk the murals, placed in the lunettes, teach that honest labor carried out in proper season brings prosperity and contentment. The medieval costumes

The Law Library: Elizabeth Dolan, 1930

The second mural commissioned for the Nebraska State Capitol is the work of a Lincoln artist, Elizabeth Dolan (circa 1884–1948). Her mural, "The Spirit of the

Prairie," was installed in 1930 (figure 6.6). It occupies the north wall above the main entrance to the Law Library. Because this space is well illuminated by natural light flooding through high-ceilinged windows on the east and west sides of the reading room, it offers what is probably the best location for a mural in the entire capitol.

Dolan chose as her subject a prairie mother as the exemplar of the prairie spirit. Accompanied by her young son and their pet dog, the woman holds her baby in her arms. She stands on a knoll, her skirt billowing in the wind. Her head is turned toward the east, suggesting that she might be musing on the home she left to come to Nebraska. Leonard Nelson, the author of a capitol guide published in 1931, understood her gaze to mean that the prairie mother, as though in a dream, looked eastward in order to visualize what the future could hold for her and her family.

Dolan, a native of Iowa, began her art education at the University of Nebraska and continued her studies at the Art Institute of Chicago, the Art Students League in New York, and the Fontainebleau School of Fine Arts in France. While in France she developed her specialty of mural painting and was strongly influenced by Pierre Puvis de Chavannes, one of the great modern masters of wall decoration. Puvis de Chavannes, who understood the medieval precepts about the integrity of a wall in relation to the painting placed on it, won the admiration of his contemporaries for his ability to create murals in accordance with ancient rules but without becoming a slave to them. He developed a distinctive style in which softly rounded forms are subtly manipulated through the application of muted colors. Although his style owed something to impressionism, it also draws on the eighteenth century in its reliance on blond color schemes.

In 1926, fresh from her studies in France, Dolan returned to Lincoln to paint the backgrounds for habitat displays in the University of Nebraska State Museum, housed in Morrill Hall. She habitually used a *fresco secco* technique—oil paint on dry plaster—which seemed well suited for her use of pale colors applied with broad, sweeping brush strokes. Her work in Morrill Hall led directly to her capitol commission and to other work in public buildings (including New York's American Museum of Natural History) and private homes in Lincoln.

Dolan's mural in the Law Library clearly reflects her training and her earlier successes. The predominantly earth-tone colors blend well with the honey marble wainscot of the lower walls and the dark oak woodwork used throughout the room. When examined at close range, her mural has the appearance of paint splashed on the wall in a rather haphazard way. But when it is observed from below, its colors and brush strokes unite to create an impression of solidity. Generally, her painting infuses the reading room with an atmosphere of warmth and light.

The Rotunda: Kenneth Evett, 1956

Two decades were to pass before the Nebraska legislature in 1949 again appropriated funds to continue the capitol mural program. Governor Val Peterson was authorized to appoint a mural commission; he chose as its head Colonel Harry Cunningham, who had played an important role in supervising the construction of the capitol. The commission announced a competition for a series of murals in the rotunda. The winner was Kenneth Evett (1913–), a professor of art in the College of Architecture at Cornell University. A native of Colorado, he attended Colorado State University and later the Kansas City Art Institute. Evett required eighteen months to complete his three murals, which were painted on canvas in his studio.

Unlike Augustus Tack and Elizabeth Dolan, whose murals represented a continuation of nineteenth-century aesthetics, Evett sought to solve the problems of architectural decoration through a more contemporary approach. Rather than relying on stylized realism, he turned toward abstraction. In doing so, he conformed to a tendency to flatten pictorial space. Since the advent of the Pre-Raphaelites in nineteenth-century England, artists tended to decrease their reliance on the representation of deep space to create pictorial effects. Similarly, the French Impressionists, with their penchant for colors of high intensity, tended to compress space. Later, twentieth-century abstract painters gave up all efforts to represent depth on a flat surface. Others declared that it was aesthetically offensive even to try. This tendency presented figurative artists with a dilemma. They could either abandon their style or run the risk of being declared anachronistic.

The muralists of the capitol sought to resolve the problem of perspective through various stylistic and technical means. Tack flattened his figures by limiting the range of color gradations between dark and light. Dolan limited the number of colors on her palette and used an open, free technique to contain her work within a two-dimensional range. Evett resolved the problem by designing compositions based on flat, geometrically abstracted figures.

The subject prescribed by Alexander for the three wall spaces in the rotunda was to represent the occupations of Nebraskans. On the east wall is "Labors of the Head," which depicts the scientific pursuits of the biologist, mathematician, designer, geologist, and paleontologist. "Labors of the Heart," which occupies the west wall, honors the arts with portrayals of musi-

6.7: "Labors of the Heart," by Kenneth Evett, west wall of the rotunda.

cians, dancers, poets, and sculptors (figure 6.7). The south panel treats "Labors of the Hand" and recognizes the manual labor of machinists, builders, and miners, as well as cattlemen and farmers.

All the figures in each of the murals are drawn in a flat, highly stylized manner. If Tack's murals may be characterized as Gothic, Evett's may be called Byzantine. His two-dimensional figures are reminiscent, for example, of the frieze of mosaic saints that adorn the nave of the Byzantine Church of San Apollinare Nuovo in Ravenna, Italy. In each case, frontal figures rely on geometric shapes to establish their forms. Evett's painting style is the most architectonic of the several in the capitol, hence his murals are for many viewers the most pleasing. They harmonize easily with both Goodhue's designs for the stone capitals and balustrades and with the mosaics by Hildreth Meiere that decorate the floor and dome of the rotunda.

The Vestibule: James Penney, 1963

The first murals that visitors see when they enter the capitol through the main entrance are a series painted by James Penney (1910–). This set of three paintings was commissioned by the same committee created by legislative action in 1949. By this time, however, the chairman was Fred N. Wells, a Lincoln merchant with a keen interest in the arts.

Penney, a native of St. Joseph, Missouri, attended the University of Kansas and graduated in 1931 with a degree in art. He subsequently studied at the Art Students League in New York. He was a member of the National Society of Mural Painters and taught art at the University of Kansas, Vassar College, Hamilton College, and other schools.

Penney's task was to connect the murals of the vestibule with the decorations of the exterior. Above the main entrance on the outside, a bas-relief sculpture depicts a pioneer family traveling with their ox-drawn Conestoga wagon to a new home in Nebraska. After viewing this exterior panel, the visitor to the capitol passes directly into the vestibule, where the murals continue the narrative.

On the west wall of the vestibule, Penney painted a

6.8: "The First Furrow," by James Penney, above the north entrance to the vestibule.

mural that shows a pioneer family camping out at the site of their new homestead. On the north side above the main entrance the settler is shown breaking the sod with a team of oxen pulling a walking plow (figure 6.8). The story is completed with the mural on the east wall, where neighbors are depicted coming to assist the settlers as they build their first home on the plains.

Stylistically, Penney's murals are executed in a broad-stroked, freely applied manner that is similar to the technique Elizabeth Dolan employed. When the mural commissioners selected Penney twenty-five years after Dolan completed her work, they inadvertently established a stylistic and a thematic unity between the north and south ends of the building.

The Foyer: Six Mosaic Murals by Four Artists in the 1960s

The last area in the capitol to receive mural decorations was the foyer, the broad corridor that connects the vestibule with the rotunda. Divided into three groin-vaulted bays, the foyer contains spaces for six murals below the clerestory windows, three on each side. The murals of the foyer were commissioned and executed in the 1960s, with the final panel installed in 1967.

At an early stage in their deliberations, the members of the Mural Commission decided that the murals in the foyer should be mosaics instead of the usual paintings or frescoes. By this means they hoped to compensate for the low level of natural light that is admitted into the space by the clerestory windows, which consist of thin onyx panels set in marble frames and which create an ambience like that in the interior of a Byzantine church. The commissioners reasoned that the reflective surfaces of glass and tile pieces might intensify the light in the corridor. They were further encouraged by a revival of mosaic techniques in the 1950s. A notable example is the west façade of Lin-

coln's Pershing Auditorium, which is almost entirely covered by a mosaic design.

The use of mosaics—small pieces of colored stones, pebbles, or glass in the creation of designs for floors or walls—is as ancient as the use of paint. The oldest technique of mosaic making involves the setting of colored materials, piece by piece and section by section, into wet cement called mud. Later, during the Renaissance, when mosaics were designed to emulate paintings on canvases, artists encountered difficulties in setting tiles of the right color and shape in place before the mud hardened. As a solution to this problem, they sketched line drawings, called cartoons, on large sheets of paper. Working in their studios, artists could then glue their colored materials onto the paper. The next step was to move sections of the design to the site of the mural, where they were tamped, face down, into the wet cement. After the mud dried, the paper was washed off, leaving the finished design in place.

According to Hartley Burr Alexander's decorative scheme, the theme in the foyer was to commemorate history: "The Life of Man on the Soil of Nebraska." The topic of the northernmost bay is the past, the central bay is reserved for the present, and the southern bay is dedicated to the future. In each case, the iconography begins at the ceiling with a mosaic medallion of a sibyl set in the center of each vault. The figure writing on a tablet in the north bay represents "Traditions of the Past"; in the center vault a woman holding a distaff represents "Life of the Present"; at the southern end a figure holds a crystal ball to symbolize "Ideals of the Future" (see figure 5.9). In harmony with this encompassing plan, each of the six murals are intended to develop a theme or an episode in Nebraska history.

The first mural, located on the east wall of the northernmost bay, commemorates "The First United States Survey" (figure 6.9). It is directly related to the mosaics designed by Hildreth Meiere on the faces of the arch above, which represent the pioneer home builder on the north and the pioneer family on the south. The survey created a systematic method for determining property lines; it was necessary before government lands could pass into private ownership. The imaginary grid formed by the United States survey also was used to determine the boundaries of counties, townships, and municipalities.

The artist chosen to depict the survey was Charles Clement, a potter from Tucson, Arizona. His mural includes representations of both governmental subdivisions in Nebraska, including the state's ninety-three counties, and geographic areas. To represent the latter, Clement created a rich composition of forms. On the right, they can be read as farming and industry in the eastern part of the state. Below and to the left, a wide band of blue tiles and forms representing plants define the Platte River valley. Above the valley is a uniformly green area representative of the Sand Hills. Across the top of the panel tan and brown forms suggest the Pine Ridge and Badlands region of Nebraska. Because commercial tiles would not allow Clement the gradations in color that he wanted for his design, he made about one-third of them himself, a task that, as a potter, he could readily assume. This skill allowed him to achieve a subtlety reminiscent of the richness that characterizes ancient mosaics.

Opposite Clement's mural in the north bay is "The Blizzard of '88," designed by Jeanne Reynal (1903–1983). Like "The First United States Survey," it is related to the Meiere designs in the arch above, which commemorate education by representing a student on the left and a teacher with a young pupil on the right

(figure 6.10). In her mural, Reynal celebrates the heroic deed of a brave teacher who led her pupils to safety during the most famous blizzard in the history of the state. By tying the children together with a clothesline and leading them to safety, she saved them from certain death. Reynal represents this relationship with a wavering line of gold tiles that stretches diagonally across the mural. The blizzard itself is personified by a female figure whose white sleeves billow outward across the upper part of the panel. The schoolchildren, rendered as stick figures, are irregularly attached to the golden rope like tumbleweeds caught in a barbed-wire fence. The teacher's cloak forms a winglike shape that suggests her role as a guardian angel.

Reynal was born in White Plains, New York, was privately educated, and made frequent trips to Europe with her family. In 1929 she met Boris Anrep, a prominent mosaicist who had recently completed a set of elegant mosaic floors in a cubist style for the British Museum. Fascinated by his craft, Reynal worked with Anrep until 1939. With the outbreak of World War II, she returned to New York, where she associated with the famous European émigré artists (such as Ferdinand Leger and Max Ernst) and their American followers, who created the Abstract Expressionist movement that dominated the postwar years.

Reynal established many innovations in the design and execution of mosaics, some of which can be seen in "The Blizzard of '88." For example, she customarily used a geologist's hammer to shatter rectangular pieces of Venetian glass tiles into jagged bits that she then scattered over a wet cement surface. This technique, which was inspired by Jackson Pollock's method of dripping paint on a canvas, can be recognized in the bits of clear glass that glitter like snow-

6.9: "The First United States Survey," by Charles Clement, foyer, north bay, east wall.

6.10: "The Blizzard of '88," by Jeanne Reynal, foyer, north bay, west wall.

flakes in the large areas of exposed black and white concrete in her mosaics. In some respects her innovations were revivals of ancient techniques. As early as the sixth century B.C., Punic peoples in Tunisia decorated concrete floors with scattered tiles and pieces of glass.

Reynal was also commissioned to execute another mural. It is on the east wall of the central bay, which memorializes "Life of the Present" (figure 6.11). In this instance her subject is "The Tree Planting" and celebrates Arbor Day, a national holiday that was started in Nebraska by J. Sterling Morton, one of the state's most distinguished leaders in the nineteenth century. As befits the celebration of a holiday, the Meiere mosaics that frame the mural are devoted to recreation: a ball player occupies the southern face of the arch and a

6.11: "The Tree Planting," by Jeanne Reynal, foyer, central bay, east wall.

6.12: "The Building of the Railroad," by Francis John Miller, foyer, central bay, west wall.

flower girl is on the north. The mural also reminds Nebraskans that the plains were treeless and that today's landscapes are the result of much tree planting. Reynal's treatment of her subject is a sumptuous composition of tree forms in Venetian glass tiles whose red, orange, yellow, gold, and blue colors shimmer in the dim light like a copse of rustling cottonwood trees.

The west wall of the central bay is dedicated to "The Building of the Railroad" (figure 6.12). Because of Nebraska's location on the Great Plains and because of its time of settlement, railroads have been central in the state's history, just as the train has been an important symbol of progress and scientific advancement.

In this sense the subject matter of this panel fits with the themes of the Meiere mosaics on the arch, which depict a student and a scientist as symbols of learning and progress.

The mural is the work of Francis John Miller (1929–), a native of London who immigrated in 1956 to Canada, where he received numerous commissions for mosaic murals. The central motif of Miller's design is a steam engine typical of nineteenth-century railroads, but the artist reminds us that the train also was important in the mythology of the Wild West. His design includes a sheriff (the figure on the extreme right wearing a large star on his lapel), a gambler (who

LAW AND ORDER
DELIVER THE SOUL
A COMMUNITY LIKE
AN INDIVIDUAL
HAS A WORK TO DO

ALL MEN ARE END·OW
ED BY THEIR CREAT
OR WITH CERTAIN
UNALIENABLE
RIGHTS · AMONG
THESE ARE · LIFE ·
LIBERTY · AND THE
PURSUIT OF
HAPPINESS

wears a black hat), and a gunfighter (in the center of the composition) who is a montage of symbols derived from playing cards and games of chance.

Both panels of the south bay were designed by Reinhold Marxhausen (1922–). The Minnesota native received his formal art education at Mills College in California and has been a professor of art at Concordia College in Seward, Nebraska, since 1952. For his designs, Marxhausen employed a distinctive technique. Whereas the other muralists constructed their designs by means of traditional techniques, he laid his tiles on plywood panels and glued them in place with epoxy. He did not limit himself to ceramic and glass

tesserae, but also incorporated pieces of hardwood flooring into his mural. In all cases, he butted the pieces tightly against each other, thereby eliminating the need for grout to fill the interstices.

"Building the Capitol" is the title of the mural that occupies the southernmost wall space on the east side of the foyer (figure 6.13). The last of the murals to be installed, it draws on well-developed principles of mural design that permit diverse elements to be arranged on a single pictorial plane. In this instance, the second capitol of Nebraska stands below and to the left of a framed quotation from the Declaration of Independence. To the right one sees an indistinct outline of

6.13: "Building the Capitol," by Reinhold Marxhausen, south bay, east wall.

6.14: "The Spirit of Nebraska," by Reinhold Marxhausen, south bay, west wall.

the present capitol. Together these elements dominate the composition and are joined in a rich field of variously colored tiles laid in purely abstract patterns.

"The Spirit of Nebraska," which occupies the south panel on the west wall, is the thematic climax of the series (figure 6.14). Because its content was not specified in Alexander's grand plan, it presented the artist with a difficult compositional problem. Marxhausen chose to treat this abstract subject through a collage of naturalistic elements and symbolic devices. The panel is dominated by a bold Arabic numeral *1* made of gold glass set in a raised square of dark wood. It symbolizes Nebraska's unicameral legislature, the only one-house state legislature in the United States.

The lower part of the panel is dominated by an overall brown color, which, according to Marxhausen, represents both the rich soil of Nebraska and the deeply rooted conservatism of its citizens. Buried in this earth are fossils of Paleolithic creatures that roamed the plains before the Ice Age. Buried with them is a black box containing human bones. They are meant to symbolize the remains of unimaginative, nonproductive people, who, in Marxhausen's view, deserve to be fossilized along with dinosaurs. But from this dark base emerge two vital elements. A plant on the left stands for agriculture, and on the right is the Nebraska capitol, itself a symbol of the spirit of Nebraska. Marxhausen's design also includes hands that are

kneading bread (to represent work) and hands that are upraised (to indicate hope and aspiration).

In some respects the murals of Marxhausen, like those of Clement and Miller, derive much of their character from the precedents established by the Mexican muralists Diego Rivera, David Siquieros, and José Clemente Orozco. In their work, and, in the United States, in the murals of Thomas Hart Benton, the traditions of pre-Renaissance art were revived, making it possible for common people, including the illiterate, to interpret what for them was common visual experience.

All the murals of the foyer were intended by Hartley Burr Alexander to illuminate the past, present, and future of Nebraska. The four artists who executed the six mosaics in this dimly lit space created for it brilliant color and high decoration. Thus, they successfully served both artistic and commemorative purposes.

Memorial Hall: Mosaics to Come

Four decades passed between the installation in 1927 of Augustus Tack's murals in the Governor's Suite and the completion of Reinhold Marxhausen's mosaic murals in 1967. During those years American art passed through many stylistic developments. The murals of the Nebraska State Capitol present in microcosm the evolution that occurred from Tack's historicism to Reynal's abstract expressionism. And yet the project remains incomplete. High in the tower is Memorial Hall, an octagonal room dedicated to the memory of Nebraskans who gave their lives in some form of service to their country. In this room eight spaces remain to be filled with murals. The Nebraska legislature has taken the steps necessary to complete the mural program. Soon the development of mural art will extend even further to include a style yet unknown.

Landscape architecture, although the least-permanent element in the total design for any building, is nevertheless an integral and important component. From the outset, the art of the landscapist was considered to be an essential part of the Nebraska capitol project. Thomas Kimball, in his statement calling for the collaboration of artists in the planning of the capitol, explicitly included the landscapist as a member of the team. Like the sculptor and the painter, the landscapist was to work under the guidance and control of the architect.

That point of view received the full endorsement of Bertram Goodhue, the architect, even though he gave only routine thought to the problem as he prepared his plans for the competition to select the architect for the new structure. Influenced by the principles of the Ecole des Beaux-Arts, Goodhue would have participated fully and enthusiastically in the integration of the landscapist's work into the large plan had he lived through the period in the early 1930s when the landscape work was completed.

Landscape Architecture, Lincoln, and the Capitol

Like the other architects in the competition, Goodhue was fully cognizant of the significant developments that occurred in the art of landscaping in the United States during the nineteenth century. One of the great events in the history of landscape architecture in the United States was the competition for a formal plan for Central Park in New York City in 1857. The winners of this competition, Frederick Law Olmsted and Calvert Vaux, were the first to use the terms *landscape architect* and *landscape architecture*. Their work contributed much to the idea that this field demanded special expertise and that it was a discipline separate from architecture.

7.1: Bronze statue of Abraham Lincoln (1912) by Daniel Chester French, and the Lincoln Monument by architect Henry Bacon, in front of the west entrance to the capitol. French and Bacon also collaborated on the Lincoln Memorial in Washington, D.C.

Questions regarding the relationship of site to monumental architecture did not originate with artists, such as Olmsted and Vaux, nor were those persons connected in any direct way with the history of the Nebraska State Capitol. But their influence was felt by city planners in mid–nineteenth century, the very time that Lincoln was platted in 1867. Like the national capital of Washington but unlike most state capitals in America, Lincoln was designated as the site of the statehouse before it had come into existence as a city. The original plat of the city shows a tract of four city blocks southeast of the emerging business district as the location of the new building. Like Capitol Hill in Washington, this site offered the highest elevation in the immediate vicinity. Its selection demonstrates that the city fathers and the first capitol commission were concerned about questions that engage landscape architects. It is not a surprise that each of Nebraska's three capitols has been erected on this prominent site.

Still, early photographs of Lincoln do not reveal great concern about landscaping as a way to soften the bleak, windswept character of the Nebraska plains. Trees were not native to the environment, and in those years technology permitted the transplanting of trees that were rarely more than three or four feet high. But the determination to supply what nature had not became almost an obsession in Nebraska, which styled itself as the Tree-Planter State in the nineteenth century.

The first state capitol faced west, a fact of importance for later landscaping considerations (see figure 1.3). It was very badly constructed, and within a decade it was apparent to everyone that it would have to be rebuilt. The second capitol, erected during the 1880s, was constructed piecemeal, first as an addition and later as a replacement for the original structure.

One result of this drawn-out process was that the main entrance of the second capitol was shifted to the north side, thereby establishing an enduring precedent (see figure 1.4).

The landscape plan for the second capitol was straightforward. It incorporated a symmetrical sidewalk system, and it had a driveway system that gave vehicular access to the east and west wings. This arrangement also provided a convenient place for statuary. In 1909 the eminent American sculptor Daniel Chester French was commissioned by the citizens of Lincoln to create a statue of Abraham Lincoln for placement on the west side of the capitol square, where it remains to this day (figure 7.1). Dedicated in 1912, this monument thus became part of the landscape environment. In the same year, the city of Lincoln constructed a series of medians in the center of Fifteenth Street, running south from the capitol square to A Street, a distance of seven blocks. This action was the first gesture by the municipal government to integrate the capitol and its site into the city landscape. Such were the conditions that existed when the capitol competition was undertaken.

Landscaping and the Capitol Commission

In January 1920 the Capitol Commission approved and distributed to the competitors the program for the capitol design. Guided by Thomas Kimball, the commissioners were remarkably free in their directives. "As to plan, scope, style, type, or material," read the program statement, "the Capitol Commissioners will offer no suggestion. Even in the matter of tradition it is clearly the desire of the Commission that each competitor shall feel free to express what is in his heart, unmindful of what has been inherited in this regard, willing even that the legacies of the Masters should

7.2: Centennial Mall, which extends north from the capitol to the Nebraska State Historical Society building.

guide and restrain rather than fetter." Beyond that, the commissioners merely added a few comments on the climate and noted that the design of the capitol should take French's statue of Lincoln into consideration. The document thus specified almost nothing that related directly to the task of the landscape architect.

The question of directional orientation of the capitol became a problem for Goodhue, the winning competitor. In his original designs, Goodhue proposed changing the orientation from the north to the west. This led him to suggest further that the Lincoln statue be placed across the street so that it might face the west side of the capitol. It was to be part of an esplanade that was to stretch westward on J Street to what is today the County-City Building on Tenth Street. In Goodhue's scheme, this arrangement would make it possible for both the Lincoln statue and the front of the capitol (with its engaged sculpture) to have the best benefits of the sun. Both needed an east-west orientation: the statue would get the morning sun; the main entrance would get the sun in the afternoon and evening. The commissioners, however, were adamant in their opposition to Goodhue's idea. They insisted that the grand portal remain on the north side. French's statue, meanwhile, has remained in its original position, where it is not as well integrated into the design as it might have been, had Goodhue got his way.

During the first fifty years of its existence, the capitol square had been planted with more than a hundred trees. By 1920, many had grown to be impressively large. Although residents of the neighborhood objected to their destruction, there was no alternative, given the size of the new structure. They simply could not be made part of the new landscape design and hence had to be destroyed.

The Capitol Environs Committee

The city of Lincoln, of course, was not oblivious to what was going on in the capitol square. There was much interest in making improvements in the city environment. In 1927 the Capitol Environs Committee developed a series of well-considered recommendations, some of which have been realized.

The committee's first proposal was to broaden Fifteenth Street to create what in recent years has become Centennial Mall. By extending northward from the capitol to R Street, the mall provides a grand prospect to link the statehouse to the state university (figure 7.2). Today, however, the view is terminated, not by the university, but by the headquarters of the Nebraska State Historical Society, which was erected on university grounds after World War II.

The committee also had recommendations for Fifteenth Street as it leads south of the capitol square. This is where in 1912 the city created a series of medians to invest the southern vista with a parklike atmosphere. The committee urged that Fifteenth Street be terminated at A Street and that the future Governor's Mansion be located there, giving it a site on the south like that of the Historical Society building at the northern end of the street.

Other recommendations of the Capitol Environs Committee included the purchase of two city blocks immediately north of the square for the creation of a war-memorial park, which was to have a series of monuments honoring the veterans of America's wars in addition to French's statue of Lincoln. The committee also recommended that buildings in the city blocks facing the capitol square be limited in height to fifty-five feet and that beyond this zone (but within eight hundred feet of the square) they be restricted to one hundred feet in height.

The committee's recommendations and their partial implementation demonstrate that the city was genuinely interested in developing the capitol environs. The idea of malls extending the capitol into the city in this way has had strong support ever since the capitol was designed.

The Landscape Architect: Ernst Herman Herminghaus

In 1933, fourteen years after it was appointed, the Capitol Commission finally took formal steps to integrate the art of the landscapist into the large design. The commission advertised its needs and before the end of the year decided to assign the task to Ernst Herminghaus, who was to prepare a plan, estimate its costs, and supervise its installation.

The selection of Herminghaus as the landscape architect was as logical as it was happy. He had been born in 1890, the fourth of five children in a German immigrant family. His father was a cigar manufacturer in Lincoln. Ernst was the only one of four brothers who had the opportunity to attend the University of Nebraska, where he was strongly attracted by the study of horticulture. He demonstrated an early interest in the theory of landscape architecture and the use of appropriate plant materials in landscape designs; he even had two articles in this field published while he was still a student. He was particularly concerned about the selection of plants that would do well in Nebraska's climate.

In addition to his horticultural interests, Herminghaus had demonstrated talents in drawing and draftsmanship, despite the handicap of blindness in one eye as the result of an accident in his high school years. He decided to further his education in landscape architecture and in 1913 was admitted as a student in the Graduate School of Design at Harvard University, which was first to offer a graduate program in landscape architecture in the United States.

At Harvard, Herminghaus readily assimilated Beaux-Arts principles of landscape architecture as espoused by Frederick Law Olmsted, Jr., and Henry Vincent Hubbard. Upon his graduation, he decided to return to Lincoln, where in autumn 1915 he opened Nebraska's first practice in landscape architecture. This enterprise was interrupted by World War I. Although his loss of sight in one eye precluded active duty in the army, he served as a planner for the construction of housing in military camps.

Herminghaus returned to Lincoln in 1920. Postwar prosperity produced a surge of growth in the construction of residences, and in 1922 the Woods Brothers Company engaged him to design the Woodshire subdivision, which is adjacent to the Lincoln Country Club between Seventeenth and Twentieth streets and north of Calvert Street. Drawing upon the ideas developed by Olmsted for Riverside, Illinois, a western suburb of Chicago, Herminghaus designed a layout with limited access and parklike areas, including circular islands at the intersections of several streets. He also introduced the concept of a privately owned open space, administered and maintained by a homeowners' association for the residents of the subdivision.

The particular space created by Herminghaus in Woodshire has special significance for the Nebraska State Capitol. A long, narrow area that envelops a modest ravine, Herminghaus's park was laid out to provide a view of the tower of the still-to-be-constructed capitol nearly two miles distant. Only after the tower had been completed at the end of the decade did this relationship become obvious to people who bought lots in the subdivision.

Herminghaus executed a similar plan in Pioneers Park, a large tract of land donated to the city of Lincoln in 1928. Located some distance west of the city beyond all residential districts, the park was intended to commemorate the accomplishments of nineteenth-century pioneers. In 1930, Herminghaus was selected to prepare a master plan for the eighty-acre park. Following classic Beaux-Arts principles, he designed entrances, circles, and other carefully controlled spatial sequences; trees were selected and placed to frame particular vistas. Again Herminghaus designed several visual allées, as they are called, that focused di-

7.3: View of the capitol from the southwest corner, showing the restoration of the visual allée as planned by Ernst Herminghaus in 1933.

rectly on the tower of Goodhue's capitol several miles distant.

Herminghaus's Plan for the Capitol Square

Finally, in 1933, Herminghaus got the opportunity to serve as the landscape architect for the capitol. Given his interests, talents, residence, and past commissions, he must have been thinking about the landscape design problems of the capitol for a decade. It is not surprising therefore that he was able quickly to produce a detailed landscape plan. But to supervise its implementation within a period of two months, as was required of him, was a phenomenal achievement. Hundreds of plants had to be selected, transported, and transplanted in a matter of weeks.

Herminghaus began with conceptual sketches that had been prepared by Oscar H. Murray, a member of the firm of Goodhue Associates. Murray's ideas were good, but they needed much development. To them Herminghaus added his own expertise regarding appropriate plant materials and their ability to survive in the Nebraska climate. The result was a plan that integrated the landscape of the square with the character of the building. He began by designing eight primary vistas around the capitol. Four were at the entrances on each side and four were directed diagonally at the pavilions or panels that decorate each corner (figure 7.3).

Herminghaus's decisions regarding ornamental trees, bushes, and shrubs were governed by the principle that plants should be secondary to the building: they should complement the building, not compete with it for attention. In his view, plant materials were to form a backdrop for the rich architectural details that grace the entrances and corners of the capitol. He therefore chose combinations of coniferous trees

along the foundations; elsewhere on the capitol grounds he selected deciduous trees for shading and accenting purposes (figure 7.4). He avoided the use of flowering plants on the exterior grounds, although he did not hesitate to use certain deciduous trees that flower in season.

One of the landscaping problems recognized by Goodhue was that the capitol was a bit too large for its site. He thus thought it would be necessary to enhance the visual effects at the entrances of the building by landscaping the site and developing axial malls that lead to each of the four entrances. Her-

7.4: The Nebraska State Capitol shortly after its completion in April, 1934, showing the original landscaping as designed by Ernst Herminghaus.

7.5: Scaled row of conifers at the south entrance, showing Herminghaus's creation of a false perspective to enhance the perceived distance between the capitol and the street.

minghaus resolved this problem by designing two scaled rows of conifers for both the north and south entrances (figure 7.5). Actually, his purpose was to create a false perspective. Twenty feet high at the street, these trees progressively decrease in height to fourteen feet at the building. In this way he caused the trees to create the illusion of a distance greater than it actually was—something that rows of trees of uniform height could not accomplish. Contemporary efforts to restore Herminghaus's design have successfully incorporated this ingenious device.

Because Herminghaus had to work under an ex-

7.6: Architect's drawing by Austin Whittlesey, a Goodhue associate, of one of the interior courtyards, showing that Goodhue intended it to contain a fountain.

7.7: The northwestern interior courtyard, 1927.

traordinarily tight schedule, he sometimes had difficulty acquiring the plants he wanted. He managed to get all the major nurseries in eastern Nebraska to cooperate and supply needed plants. He also went to the citizens of Lincoln and Omaha and asked them to donate, or sell at minimal cost, specific trees that he wanted for his design. The response was enthusiastic.

In accordance with Goodhue's intentions, Herminghaus planned to place tall, columnar conifers—like the well-known Italian cypresses—along the walls of the capitol to punctuate the strong foundation line of the building. His solution was to install eastern red cedars that were to be pruned into the strongly vertical or pinnacle shape of the Italian cypress. Unfortunately, native cedars will quickly revert to their normally wide shape if not maintained properly. Present-day restoration efforts have therefore diverged from Herminghaus's specifications in this instance and a new variety, a hybrid juniper that is true to his intentions but was unavailable at the time, has been substituted for native cedar.

The Interior Courtyards

Herminghaus's plans for the four interior courtyards are much different from the exterior. Intended as retreats for state employees and visitors to the capitol, the courtyards were to be the delightful showcases of his design, unusually rich in the diversity of flowers, small trees and shrubs. Whereas Herminghaus intended the exterior to be landscaped in a subtle, understated fashion, the interior spaces were to provide a diversity of color.

The architectural design of the courtyards is repetitive. Each has a walk system composed of a circle within a rectangle, the corners of which are connected diagonally with the circle (figure 7.6). According to the original plan, there was to be a fountain at the center of each circle, but it was never completed. The walks are paved with flagstones; borders consist of marble and slate tiles that were retrieved from the rotunda floor of the previous capitol. The walks define planting beds that are bordered by privet hedges. Perennial flowers, according to Herminghaus's plan, were planted in each bed and each courtyard received a different floral variety. The beds on the outer perimeters were planted with a wide variety of ornamental shrubs and trees, all of which provided brilliant color (figure 7.7).

Unfortunately, Herminghaus's courtyard gardens were not maintained and within ten years they had fallen into disrepair and neglect.

Efforts at Restoration

Trees, shrubs, and flowers, both annual and perennial, have lives of their own. Plants grow, are subject to disease, and die. They must be fed, watered, and otherwise cared for. Unless the art of the landscapist is respected through appropriate maintenance efforts, the finest designs will quickly deteriorate. That is precisely what happened to Herminghaus's landscaping. Today one can only imagine the artistry with which his plantings were once invested. Herminghaus himself was grieved by their gradual deterioration and personally spent hours in a vain effort to sustain his design. But the magnitude of the task exceeded the means at hand.

The state government of Nebraska has undertaken a program of restoration, not only in the landscape architecture, but in other changes that have been made in the original capitol plans. It is likely that someday Nebraskans will be able to view their statehouse as it was intended by the company of artists—architect, symbologist, sculptor, mosaicist, muralist, and landscapist—who conceived its splendor. The art of the landscapist, which is the most ephemeral, is also comparatively easy to restore. In the decades that have passed since Herminghaus completed his task, much landscape material has been inappropriately placed. Because the records reveal the details of Herminghaus's design, it is possible to restore the plants in their intended places as specified and thus to respect the integrity of Herminghaus's art.

The following list is adapted from the document prepared by Hartley Burr Alexander in which he specified the ideas and the subject matter of the sculptures and murals of the capitol. It is generally limited to subject matter treated in this book. It does not include inscriptions.

I. Exterior Iconography.

All sculptures were designed by Lee Lawrie.

A. North Portal: The Spirit of Law as Shown in History

1. Stairway: Foundations of Life on the Prairies. Four bas-relief panels depicting bison, two of bulls and two of cows with calves.

2. Doorway: The Spirit of the Pioneers (bas-relief panel)

3. Pylon: Guardians of the Law. Engaged figures of Wisdom, Justice, Power, and Mercy, with arms of the United States of America and the state of Nebraska.

B. South Pavilion: Written and Constitutional Law

1. Great Legislators of the Western World (engaged sculptures).

a. Hammurabi

b. Moses

c. Akhnaton

d. Solon

e. Solomon

f. Julius Caesar

g. Justinian

h. Charlemagne

i. Napoleon

j. Minos

2. Great Historical Documents (bas-relief panels on the balustrade).

a. The Declaration of Independence

b. The Magna Carta

c. The Constitution of the United States

C. Terrace Circuit: Moments in the History of Law. This series of eighteen panels summarizes the history of law in our civilization. It begins on the north side of the northeast corner of the capitol. Nine panels are on the west side and commemorate events from ancient history. A second set of nine panels are on the east side and treats events from English and American history. Three panels (numbers 3, 4, and 5) are integrated into the design for the east entrance. Similarly, the panels of the west entrance (numbers 13, 14, and 15) are also parts of the series. The series ends on the north side of the northeast corner of the capitol.

1. Moses Bringing the Law from Mount Sinai

2. Deborah Judging Israel

3. The Judgment of Solomon

4. Solon Giving a New Constitution to Athens

5. Publishing the Law of the Twelve Tables in Rome

6. Establishing the Tribunate of the People

7. Plato Writing His Dialogue on the Ideal Republic

8. Orestes before the Areopagites

9. The Codification of Roman Law under Justinian

10. The Codification of Anglo-Saxon Law under Ethelbert

11. Milton Defending Free Speech before Cromwell

12. Burke Defending America in Parliament

13. Las Casas Pleading the Cause of the Indian

14. Signing the Pilgrim Compact on the Mayflower

15. Lincoln's Emancipation Proclamation

16. The Purchase of Louisiana from Napoleon

17. The Kansas-Nebraska Act

18. Admission of Nebraska as a State in the Union

D. The Tower.

1. The Base: The Course of Human Civilization (engaged sculptures, two on each side, beginning on the north, right side).

a. The Dawn of History—Pentaour, an Egyptian scribe.

b. Cosmic Tradition—Ezekiel, a Semitic seer.

c. The Birth of Reason—Socrates, a Greek philosopher.

d. The Reign of Law—Marcus Aurelius, a Roman emperor.

e. The Glorification of Faith—the Apostle John.

f. The Age of Chivalry—King Louis IX of France.

g. The Discovery of Nature—Isaac Newton, a Renaissance scientist.

h. The Liberation of Peoples—Abraham Lincoln, the Emancipator.

2. The Dome

a. Eight thunderbird designs in blue, red, and yellow mosaic tiles provide the platform for the dome, which is covered with gold tiles.

b. The Sower. A nineteen-foot image made of bronze and resting on a thirteen-foot-high pedestal, this monumental statue represents the foundation of the life of man in agriculture.

II. The Interior Decorations

A. The Vestibule: Gifts of Nature to Man on the Plains of Nebraska.

1. The Ceiling. Mosaics by Hildreth Meiere.

a. Crown of the dome: The Symbol of the Sun.

b. First concentric: The Four Seasons and the Signs of the Zodiac.

c. Second concentric: The First Fruits of the Soil (cattle, sheep, swine, maize, wheat, grasses, fruit, and flowers).

d. Four pendentives: Plowing, Sowing, Cultivating, Reaping.

2. The Floor: Mosaics by Hildreth Meiere represent the cosmic sun encircled by geometric patterns of other celestial forms. The entire composition symbolizes Creation.

3. The Walls: Three murals by James Penney.

a. West wall: The Homesteader's Campfire.

b. North wall: The First Furrow.

c. East wall: The House Raising.

B. The Foyer. This great hall is divided into three sections that sequentially represent the Past, Present, and Future of the Life of Man on the Soil of Nebraska. The mosaics are by Hildreth Meiere.

1. The Ceiling: Three tondi with sibylline figures:

a. Traditions of the Past.

b. Life of the Present.

c. Ideals of the Future.

2. The Floor:

a. The Spirit of the Soil, symbolic of the Earth and its foundations of rock.

b. The Spirit of Vegetation, with flower and tree forms.

c. The Spirit of Animal Life, depicted as a guardian of animals.

3. The Walls: Six murals.

a. East wall, north bay: The First United States Survey, by Charles Clement.

b. West wall, north bay: The Blizzard of '88, by Jeanne Reynal.

c. East wall, central bay: The Tree Planting, by Jeanne Reynal.

d. West wall, central bay: The Building of the Railroad, by Francis John Miller.

e. East wall, south bay: Building the Capitol, by Reinhold Marxhausen.

f. West wall, south bay: The Spirit of Nebraska, by Reinhold Marxhausen.

C. The Rotunda: Mosaics by Hildreth Meiere.

1. The Dome: The Virtues of the State: Temperance, Courage, Justice, Wisdom, Magnanimity, Faith, Hope, Charity.

2. The Floor. The mosaics here are symbolically connected to those of the foyer.

a. Entrance panel: Genius of Creative Energy.

b. Central panel: Earth as Life-Giver (Mother Nature).

c. Four surrounding nodes are representations of four geologic ages, the genii of Water, Fire, Air, and Earth.

3. The Murals. By Kenneth Evett.

a. East wall: Labors of the Head.

b. West wall: Labors of the Heart.

c. South wall: Labors of the Hand.

D. The Governor's Suite. Murals by Augustus Vincent Tack.

1. Reception Room: The State, Its Citizens, and Activities of Life.

a. West wall: Equality before the Law. The state as protector of the sick and helpless; the state as provider of learning: Philosophy, Science, and Art.

b. East wall: Understanding, Justice, and Mercy, with citizens on either side; symbols of civilizations from which American codes of law are derived.

c. South wall: The rights of free speech, religious freedom, and universal suffrage.

2. Governor's Office.

a. Center of the dome: The four seasons represented by separate figures.

b. Lunettes formed by the pendentives that support the dome: Here the seasons are represented by four murals: Tilling the Soil (Spring); Cultivation of the Soil (Summer); Harvest Season (Fall); and Winter River God and Rewards of the Harvest (Winter).

E. The Law Library: The major decorative feature of this room is a mural, The Spirit of the Prairie, by Elizabeth Dolan.

Other spaces within the capitol include important decorative elements. Chief among them are the Supreme Court Chamber, which contains three large tapestries, the Legislative Chamber (west) and the old Senate Chamber (east). The ceiling of the latter offers four magnificent mosaics on Indian themes done by Hildreth Meiere.

The huge doors that open into the legislative chambers are particularly dramatic. Opposite each other in the rotunda, these two creations symbolize the idea of the Tree of Life, as expressed in both Indian and Euroamerican cultural traditions. On the east side, leading into the old Senate Chamber, Indian symbolism emphasizes the importance of corn (see p. vi, opposite the table of contents). On the west side, at the entrance to the Legislative Chamber, Assyrian models are used to stress the centrality of trees and their cultivation in Western civilization (p. 114).

Published materials on the Nebraska State Capitol vary considerably in character and quality. All of the chapters in this book rely upon them to some extent. The most thorough and readily available study is Eric Scott McCready, "The Nebraska State Capitol: Its Design, Background, and Influence," *Nebraska History* 55 (Fall 1974): 325–461. This extended article was originally a doctoral dissertation at the University of Delaware.

Elinor L. Brown, *Architectural Wonder of the World: Nebraska's State Capitol Building* (Ceresco, Neb.: Midwest Publishing Co., 1965) is also useful. In addition to several pages on the "History of Nebraska's Houses of State" (pp. 129–37), it includes a rich inventory of photographs of the present capitol.

Other general books on the capitol include an early guidebook by Leonard Nelson, *Nebraska's Memorial Capitol* (Lincoln: Woodruff, 1931), and a brief introduction by Harry F. Cunningham, *The Capitol, Lincoln, Nebraska: An Architectural Masterpiece* (Lincoln: Johnsen, 1954). An architect who came to Lincoln as a member of the Goodhue architectural firm, Cunningham remained in Lincoln to assist in the founding of the architectural program in the University of Nebraska.

A special issue of *American Architect* published in October 1934 is a particularly valuable source of information about the design and construction of the capitol. It also offers a treasury of outstanding photographic reproductions.

Henry-Russell Hitchcock and William Seale place state capitols within the large context of architectural history in *Temples of Democracy: The State Capitols of the USA* (New York: Harcourt Brace Jovanovich, 1976). Nebraska's statehouse is treated specifically on pages 272–80.

Many other books and articles have been written about various aspects of the capitol and its history. Materials that have been particularly useful to the authors of the essays in this book are cited below by chapter.

1. The Capitals and Capitols of Nebraska

This chapter is based on published materials, including standard accounts of the history of Nebraska, such as Addison E. Sheldon, *Nebraska: The Land and the People* (Chicago: Lewis, 1931); James C. Olson, *History of Nebraska*, 2d ed. (Lincoln: University of Nebraska Press, 1966); and Dorothy Weyer Creigh, *Nebraska: A Bicentennial History* (New York: Norton, 1977).

Greater detail often may be found in histories of Omaha and Lincoln, including Lawrence H. Larsen and Barbara J. Cottrell, *The Gate City: A History of Omaha* (Boulder: Pruett, 1982); Alfred Sorenson, *The Story of Omaha from Pioneer Days to the Present Time*, 3d ed. (Omaha: National Printing Co., 1923); James L. McKee, *Lincoln, the Prairie Capital* (Woodland Hills, Calif.: Windsor, 1984); A. B. Hayes and Sam D. Cox, *History of the City of Lincoln, Nebraska* (Lincoln: State Journal, 1889); and Andrew J. Sawyer, ed.,

Lincoln, the Capital City and Lancaster County, Nebraska (Chicago: S. J. Clarke, 1916).

Some events treated only in passing here have been investigated in great detail, but the territorial period is examined with much sophistication in James B. Potts, "Nebraska Territory, 1854–1867: A Study of Frontier Politics" (Ph.D. dissertation, University of Nebraska–Lincoln, 1973). An example of a very old but still useful essay is by one of Nebraska's pioneer journalists, Charles H. Gere, "The Capital Question in Nebraska, and the Location of the Seat of Government at Lincoln," *Transactions and Reports of the Nebraska State Historical Society* 2 (1887): 63–80.

2. The Architectural Vision of Bertram Grosvenor Goodhue

Many books and articles have been published through the years that are useful in understanding the place of Bertram Goodhue and his achievements in American architectural history. For the basic historical context, one might consult John Burchard and Albert Bush-Brown, *The Architecture of America: A Social and Cultural History* (Boston: Little, Brown, 1966). Richard Oliver's biography, *Bertram Grosvenor Goodhue* (Cambridge, Mass.: MIT Press, 1983), is valuable for understanding Goodhue's personality and the context of his work.

Two articles in *American Architect* treat the seven competing plans submitted to the Capitol Commission. They are "Nebraska State Capitol Competition," *American Architect* 118 (July 21, 1920) and "Nebraska State Capitol Competition, Part II," 118 (July 28, 1920).

3. Symbolism and Inscriptions

This chapter is based primarily on unpublished manuscript materials, the most important of which are the Hartley Burr Alexander Papers in the archives of Ella

Strong Denison Library at Scripps College in Claremont, California. Other sources are the Hartley Burr Alexander collections in Love Memorial Library at University of Nebraska–Lincoln and at the Nebraska State Historical Society in Lincoln. The official records of the Nebraska Capitol Commission, including minutes and correspondence, are held in the Nebraska Capitol Commission Collection in the State Archives, Nebraska State Historical Society, Lincoln. The newspaper files at the Nebraska State Historical Society provide supplementary information. The Lee O. Lawrie Papers in the Library of Congress, Washington, D.C., are also useful.

Alexander interpreted his own scheme for the Nebraska capitol in several articles. Among them are "Prairie, Pioneer, and State: Their Symbological Interpretation," in Charles Harris Whitaker and Hartley Burr Alexander, *The Architectural Sculpture of the State Capitol at Lincoln, Nebraska* (New York: Press of the American Institute of Architects, 1926); "Nebraska's Monumental Capitol at Lincoln: Bertram Grosvenor Goodhue, Architect, Lee Lawrie Sculptor," *Western Architect* 32 (1923): 113–16; and "Symbolism and Inscriptions," *American Architect* 145 (October 1934): 24–28.

Readers may find additional information in the standard secondary sources. Eric McCready's lengthy article, cited above, includes Alexander's "Synopsis of Decorations and Inscriptions" (pp. 451–58). Several other publications, including Cunningham's booklet cited above, reiterate the interpretive scheme of the building.

4. Art, Architecture, and Humanism

An excellent inventory of the exterior sculptures of the Nebraska State Capitol and detailed background material on their subject matter is available in Orville H. Zabel's extensively illustrated article "History in Stone: The Story in Sculpture on the Exterior of the Nebraska Capitol," *Nebraska History* 62 (Fall 1981): 285–372. Other useful illustrations are found in Elinor Brown's book, cited above. Eric McCready's lengthy study includes a chapter on the sculptures of the capitol. See also Timothy J. Garvey, "Strength and Stability on the Middle Border: Lee Lawrie's Sculpture for the Nebraska State Capitol," *Nebraska History* 65 (Summer 1984): 157–78.

Other interpretations and criticisms of Lawrie's work are in Leo Friedlander, "Lee Lawrie: Limestone Panels that Endure," *National Sculpture Review* 9 (Summer 1960), and Adolph Block, Joseph Kiselewski, and Robert Wakeman, "Lee Lawrie: In Memoriam," *National Sculpture Review* 12 (Summer 1963). See also "Lee Lawrie's Sculpture for the Nebraska Capitol," *American Magazine of Art* 19 (January 1928): 13–16; Hartley Burr Alexander, "The Sculpture of Lee Lawrie," *Architectural Forum* 54 (May 1931): 587–600; and Richard Oliver, *Bertram Grosvenor Goodhue* (Cambridge, Mass.: MIT Press, 1983).

5. The Decorative Art of Hildreth Meiere

Few articles and no books have been written on Hildreth Meiere and her contribution to the art of decoration. A brief biography is found in the *National Cyclopaedia of American Biography*, current vol. D (New York: James T. White, 1934), p. 337. See also Ernest W. Watson, "Hildreth Meiere, Mural Painter," *American Artist* 5 (September 1941): 5–8, and Anne Lee, "Hildreth Meiere, Mural Painter," *Architectural Record* 62 (August 1927): 103–12. Meiere expressed some of her own views about architectural decoration

in "The Question of Decoration," *Architectural Forum* 57 (July 1932): 1–9. Hartley Burr Alexander's article, "Hildreth Meiere's Work for Nebraska," *Architecture* 63 (June 1931): 321–28, is especially helpful. Alexander makes reference to his meeting with Meiere in Siena both here and in "Symbolism and Inscriptions," *American Architect* 145 (October 1934): 24–28. An extensive photographic inventory of Meiere's Nebraska work may be found in Elinor Brown's book, cited above.

The mosaics in the Cathedral of Siena are discussed with brilliant photography in Bruno Santi, *The Marble Pavement of the Cathedral of Siena* (Florence, Italy: Scala, 1982). For excellent photographs of the mosaics in Ravenna, see Antonio Paolucci, *Ravenna: An Art Guide* (Ravenna, Italy: Scala, 1971).

6. The Capitol Murals

The general subject of mural painting has been treated in many books and articles. One might, for example, consult E. H. Gombrich, *Means and Ends: Reflections on the History of Fresco Painting* (London: Thames and Hudson, 1976), or such earlier studies as Pauline King, *American Mural Painting* (Boston: Noyes, Platt, 1902), and Nancy McClelland, *The Practical Book of Decorative Wall-Treatments* (Philadelphia: Lippincott, 1926).

Materials for understanding the murals of the Nebraska State Capitol are limited in both quantity and quality. The early guidebook by Leonard Nelson, cited above, is useful, as are official reports, such as Charles W. Bryan, *Report of Nebraska State Capitol Commission to the Fiftieth Session of the Nebraska State Legislature* (Lincoln, 1935), and contemporary articles in professional journals. Examples of the latter include "The Nebraska State Capitol," *American Ar-*

chitect 145 (October 1934), and "Nebraska Capitol Murals," *College Art Journal* 14 (Spring 1955). Newspaper articles are also informative. For examples, see the *Lincoln Sunday Journal and Star*, Jan. 15, 1956, p. 9D, and the *Lincoln Star*, Jan. 25, 1956, p. 14.

For the work of individual artists, great variation exists and ranges from such an extensive study as Dore Ashton's *The Mosaics of Jeanne Reynal* (New York: George Wittenborn, 1964) to virtually no published materials, as on Charles Clement. For Augustus Vincent Tack, see "Mural Decorations by Augustus Vincent Tack, Nebraska State Capitol," *American Magazine of Art* 19 (January 1928): 5–12, and Tack's own *Governor's Suite: Nebraska State Capitol* (Lincoln, 1928). Similarly, James Penney comments on his own work in "James Penney Discusses His Approach to Painting," *American Artist* 15 (March 1951). Brief biographical sketches on Elizabeth Dolan, Kenneth Evett, and James Penney are included in Elinor Brown, cited above.

7. Landscape Architecture

Almost nothing has been published on the landscaping of the Nebraska State Capitol, and only one article on Ernst Herminghaus has appeared. The latter is an illustrated essay by Richard K. Sutton, "Ernst H. Herminghaus, Landscape Architect," *Nebraska History* 66 (Winter 1985): 372–91.

Other sources used in the preparation of this article are in the Nebraska State Capitol Collection in the offices of the Nebraska Department of Administrative Services, State Building Division, Lincoln, Nebraska.

The Contributors: **Betsy S. Gabb** is Assistant Professor of Textiles, Clothing, and Design, University of Nebraska–Lincoln. **Norman Geske** is Director

emeritus of the Sheldon Memorial Art Gallery, University of Nebraska–Lincoln. **Dale L. Gibbs**, Professor of Architecture, University of Nebraska–

Lincoln, is a Fellow of the American Institute of Architects. **Frederick C. Luebke** is Charles J. Mach Distinguished University Professor of History, Uni-

versity of Nebraska–Lincoln. **David Murphy,** an architect at the Nebraska State Historical Society, serves as Deputy State Historic Preservation Officer.

Jon Nelson is Curator of the Center for Great Plains Studies Collection of Art, University of Nebraska–Lincoln. **Robert C. Ripley**, an architect in the

Nebraska State Department of Administrative Services, is Manager of Capitol Restoration and Promotion. **H. Keith Sawyers** is Professor of Archi-

tecture, University of Nebraska–Lincoln. **Joan Woodside** is Assistant Professor of Textiles, Clothing, and Design, University of Nebraska–Lincoln.

Grateful acknowledgment is made to the following people and institutions for the use of illustrations

Alinari/Art Resource, New York, figure 5.11; R. Bruhn, figure 4.7, and facing pages vii and 115, © 1982 by R. Bruhn; Center for Great Plains Studies, University of Nebraska–Lincoln, figures 1.1, 1.2; College of Architecture, University of Nebraska–Lincoln, figures 4.5, 4.6; David Murphy, figures 3.1, 3.2, 3.4, 3.6, 3.9, 7.1, 7.2; National Sculpture Society, New York, N.Y., figure 4.1; Nebraska State Department of Administrative Services, State Building Division, figures 3.8, 7.7; Nebraska State Department of Administrative Services, Sidney Spelts Collection, figures 3.10, 4.2, 4.4, 4.9, 5.1, 5.2, 5.5, 5.9, 5.10, 5.12, 6.1 through 6.14, 7.3; Nebraska State Historical Society, figures 1.3, 1.4, 1.5, 2.7, 2.10, 2.11, 2.13, 3.3, 3.5, 3.7, 3.11, 4.3, 4.8, 4.10, 4.11, 4.12, 4.13, 5.4, 5.6, 5.7, 5.8, 7.4, 7.5, 7.6; Scala/ Art Resource, New York, N.Y., figure 5.3; University of Chicago Archives, figure 2.8; U.S. Commission of Fine Arts, figure 2.9. Figures 2.1 through 2.6 and 2.12 are from *American Architect* 118 (July 20, 1920).

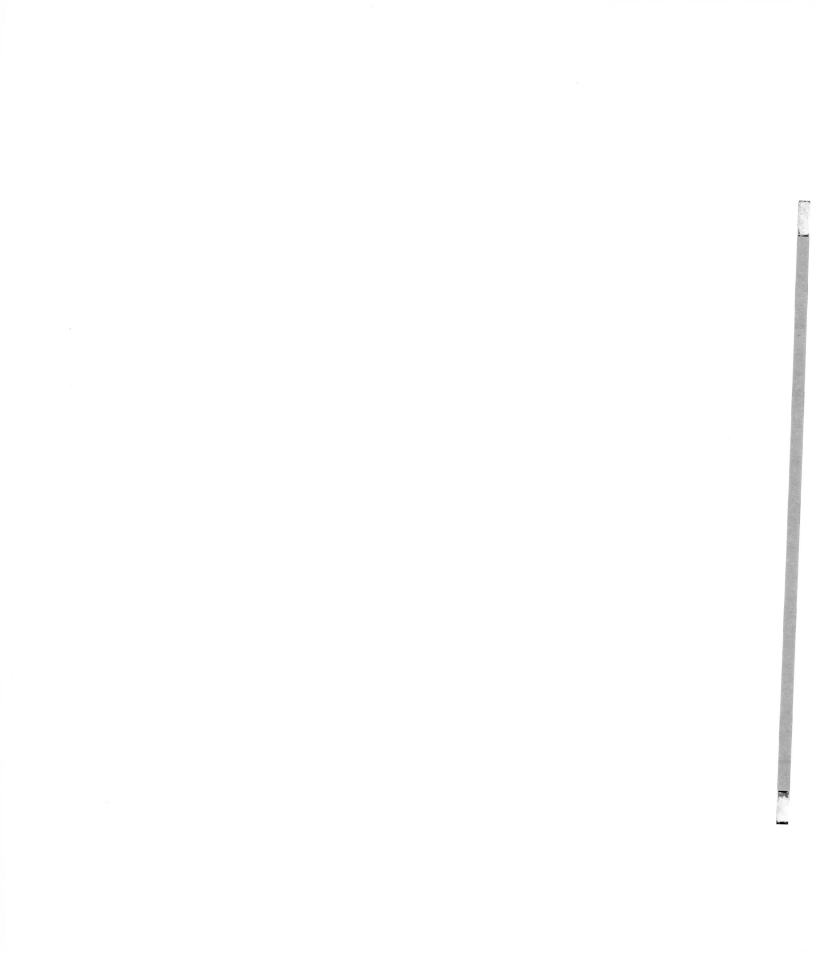